The Gospel According to a

Basket-Case

The Gospel According to a Basket-Case

a memoir

Trevor Church

napalm press ♠ los angeles

This book is a book of nonfiction. I have changed the names, certain cities and other identifying details to protect the identities of those involved and their families. This is my version of the truth as I remember it.

Saint Sophia originally published by 3 Elements Review. A version of Water Lilies appeared in The Promethean. Comfortably Numb was the recipient of the Tom and Phyllis Burnam Scholarship for Best Nonfiction.

ISBN: 978-0-578-58510-9

www.TrevorChurch.com

Cataloging-in-Publication Data

Names: Church, Trevor, 1991-author.

Title: The gospel according to a basket-case/ Trevor Church

Description: Los Angeles : Napalm Press, 2019.

Subjects: LCSH: Autobiographies—Memoirs | Biography—Mental illness | Teenagers—Mental health | Biography—Teenagers with mental disabilities | Rehabilitation—Personal narratives | Mentally ill—Personal narratives | Drug addicts— biography | Drug addicts—rehabilitation

For Gabrielle, "Hear you me my friends,
on sleepless roads, the sleepless go,
may angels lead you in"
-Jimmy Eat World

"Be young, be dope, be proud – like an American."
-Lana Del Rey

"I feel guilt, I feel guilt,
Though I know I've done no wrong I feel guilt.
I feel bad, so bad,
Though I ain't done nothing wrong I feel bad.
I feel blood, I feel blood,
Though I feel it in my veins, it's not enough.
I feel blood, I feel blood,
Though it's streaming through my veins it's not enough.
I'm like a curious child, just give me more."
-Marianne Faithfull

Contents

Saint Sophia
Los Angeles, CA – Summer 2007

She kept her cock taped between her legs
– the agony of the restrained appendage filling
with blood woke her some nights. I would lie
still, pretending not to hear the weeps from the
bathroom as she prayed for it to fall off. She once
told me that God had to exist, because only a man
was dumb enough to put her in a man's body. She
made jokes – attempts to mask the sadness. It was
this sadness that led me to constantly watch her,
believing that if I turned for a second, when I'd
go to speak again I'd only hear an echo – now
lost in the dark of her emptiness. I believed her
sorrow was this black hole that would eventually
devour everything. It was a sorrow I didn't
understand.

She'd sit for hours at her old vanity,
smoking through this long cigarette holder that
she claimed was the actual prop Audrey used
in *Breakfast at Tiffany's*. That was a lie in the real
world, but a legend in ours – Hollywood folklore
that was spread-out like the cocaine we were
doing in the back-booth of seedy Santa Monica
gay bars. I now struggle in separating most of this
folklore from fact. The few memories I possess
that I know to be authentic – those not yet tainted
by time or the drugs ingested while making them
– are now broken glass shards from that old
vanity mirror. The reflections show a sixteen-
year-old runaway watching her blow kisses at

Sophia Loren on the television. That's how she picked her name, Sophia. She, too, was a Latina bombshell. She looked a lot like her, right down to the small of her back that swayed out like she was asking for it. That's what the guys we'd walk by on La Cienega said at least. If we were far enough and had enough drinks in us, she'd hike her dress up and rear *the ugly head* at them – usually scaring them off... sometimes turning them on. Despite the humor, all I could focus on was the sadness.

I never knew details about her past or even her present. I just knew I was in Los Angeles without a place to stay. She told me she took a chance on me because no one had taken one on her. Before Sophia I didn't know Christian Dior from Christian Louboutin. I had Levi's and a few Beatles shirts, with hair to match. Sophia showed me *well-dressed*, and showed me how to get the suitors that would keep me that way. Every sidewalk was a catwalk for her. She taught me to light a cigarette while keeping a fast pace. It was important to be poise. Ironically, she's also the one that told me whenever I'm in a fight with someone much larger (this wasn't rare as I stood 5'10, barely hitting 120lbs) to always punch them in the throat.

I stayed with her on and off for two months before burning out on heroin and coke. I woke up one morning and decided to leave. I taped a note to Sophia's mirror thanking her, and telling her that one day we would both find our place – I didn't understand that for some, happiness is a pill that comes in extended release. Had my understanding of depression been accurate back then, I think I would have stayed, now understanding that the severity of one's mental illness is often contributed to by the dismissal of their words and beliefs by those around them. I try and see clearly where the lines get blurry and figure out if she had tried to tell me: If she was talking that whole time and no one listened

I think about my dance with mental illness now and try to pinpoint where it starts and where it ends. Aside from an incident involving a boy I was in kindergarten with, it always starts with Sophia – a friend who had been burned by the disorder. I went back to L.A. a few years ago and discovered that Sophia's tragedy, like most of her life, has become Hollywood folklore. Legend has it she'd gone to Venice Beach and gathered an audience as she took off her clothes, letting the flaccid, phallic object she'd kept hidden since diapers unravel – as if coming to terms with it finally. She stood at the edge of the waves, gas-can in hand and placed Audrey's cigarette holder in her mouth one last time. Scorned for so long, she'd finally decided to extinguish the fire that had been burning her. It was the same fire that was now burning me.

Our Sanctuary on Wheels
Minneapolis, MN – February 2008

Awake 49 hours.

A cloud of smoke bombarded me as I
pulled the dented, silver door open. I sat down
and became immersed in it, I became saturated in
the aroma of stale cigarettes and coffee. I
watched her – unable to see her face through the
jungle of half-dreaded, brown and red hair. Her
cigarette was burned to the filter. In her lap was
the mound of ash from what must have been an
entire cigarette. She lit 40 cigarettes a day but
only remembered to take a drag off half of them.
I gazed intently while she scrolled through her
iPod. I felt the tingling of anxiety in my gut as I
watched the delicate tremble of her fingers, as
they desperately searched for the next song to
play.

The bitch started without me. Heat rushed
to my face, turning it red in anger and jealousy.

*If I explode though, my fix for the
morning is fucked. She'll tell me to get out, and
that'll be it. Chill.*

My head was still foggy from the night
before, and my brain felt fried. I couldn't take my
eyes away from her searching fingers. Her nail
polish had been chipping off for a few weeks,
exposing the yellow stains hidden beneath the red
coat.

It was 7am, neither of us had slept, and she was playing Dub-Step. The bass sizzled through my body in one giant wave helping to drown out the anger that had filled me. She put the iPod down and picked up her phone. We were still outside my house. She looked like Medusa had Medusa resided in a meth lab, but I was still entranced by her semblance. There was something about her. She had this power to captivate. She brought the now completely extinguished cigarette to her face as she gnawed at her finger nails like a hungry dog– spitting the discolored bits into her car.

She finally hit the gas, sending us down my road through the snow storm. Still not saying a word. She dropped her phone in the cup holder so she could pull three Adderall from her pocket. She held them to my lips – still not talking to me, or looking at me. I opened wide enough to retrieve the pills, feeling a little sting as she pushed them through my cracked lips. The dry tip of my now extended tongue graced her index finger, bringing the bead-filled-capsules to the back of my mouth, accompanied by the taste of salt and nicotine from her hand. She reached down again and handed me a Red Bull. My fingers began to shake as I cracked the beverage. Soon the 90mg of Adderall would enter my system, and I'd be taken by the euphoria.

Awake 50 hours.

We turned down the road towards school. My bloodshot eyes felt the sting of the early morning sun poking through the clouds. I lit a cigarette when we parked, closing my eyes, enjoying the burn as the harsh smoke filled my aching lungs. I couldn't look at her – my now trembling hands would only get worse. I peeked from my left eye, and my jaw locked and teeth clenched: she was gently tapping small chunks of compressed white powder from a baggie onto my chemistry book. *Breathe.* I took a deep breath, shifted in my seat and reached for my wallet. I fought my anticipation, wrestling out my credit card, getting resistance from my unsteady fingers. I pulled out a $2 bill and she passed me my textbook. I covered the snow in her car with the bill and pressed my phone on top of it – I could feel the clumps of powder disperse as I pushed down on the bill. My hand stopped shaking so I could use my card to now scrape the top of the bill, making sure everything beneath was flattened. We made eye-contact for the first time as I handed her the $2 bill. She bit her lip and smiled, exposing a flake of red nail polish stuck to her tooth. Her eyebrows raised and she broke into a smile. She'd cut the tension with her smile as I cut us lines with my card. The tension that builds between tweakers before getting their fix had been broken.

The shaking in my hands started again and I struggled to divide our mountain into two even piles. It didn't help that the speaker on her side of the car was blown. The base continued to pump vibrations through the two narrow lines I'd cut, causing them to widen slightly. Without warning she leaned towards my lap with the now rolled bill. In one swift inhale her entire six-inch line was gone. When she lifted her head I snatched the rolled bill from her hand, and slowly guided it over my line, savoring the sensation. Something I had convinced myself was a religious experience.

Over time I'd come to love the bitter taste that filled my mouth shortly after doing a line. I anticipated the clumps of coke and mucus that would soon drip down my throat. I lit another Newport, letting the menthol compliment the numbing sensation that took over my mouth. Class started in an hour, leaving enough time to do a few more lines before the bell would ring, and we'd be forced to leave our safe-haven.

Awake 53.5 hours.

I'd spent the past three and a half hours stuck in various classrooms. The comedown from the coke came during my second class, and the agitation from the Adderall started in my third class. I sat staring at the clock, empty minded, waiting to be dismissed for lunch. Sure that I would die before the bell rang.

When it finally did, I hurried out to the parking lot, waiting for her. It wasn't long before I heard the intensity of her heels striking the pavement behind me. I looked up and saw her large black sunglasses sliding down her nose so she could make eye contact. She gave me a look of exhaustion as her delicate hands grappled to gain control of her coffee, cigarettes, phone, iPod and keys. It was more difficult to maintain the high mid-day during the week. Lunch meant leaving school, parking somewhere, doing a few bumps and getting back before our next class. Cigarettes lit, music on, car on, and less than thirty minutes to be back.

Awake 59 hours.

We started drinking the second we got into the car after school. We had kept our $8 vodka in water bottles, chugging them nonchalantly as we drove. We parked at a gas station so we could decide what to do. One cigarette after another, we continued to watch people enter and leave the gas station.

"We're supposed to get eight inches of snow tonight." I finally broke the silence and turned my head to her.

"Wacconia?" She responded, meeting my gaze with her melancholy expression.

Wacconia is a small farm town about an hour or so outside of the Twin Cities. We had a habit of ending up there during the week. We liked it because we'd seldom see anyone else; it was desolate. One might assume that this sort of seclusion (being in the middle of the woods alone at night) could trigger the amphetamine-fueled, sleep-deprived psychosis we were prone to. This is definitely the case, but only when we stepped out of the car; something we would only do should we needed to piss. Inside the car was different. It was our sanctuary.

Awake 61 hours.

Driving through the winding roads of the farm town, we'd found the perfect lake, surrounded by acres of woods. We pulled off the road towards the lake but as we neared the frozen bank, she slammed on the brakes and sent my euphoric high into paranoid anger.

"There are no fishing huts, do you think the ice is thick enough to drive on?" She asked, squinting her eyes in attempt to see better through the darkness and quickly falling snow.

"Jesus! Fuck! Was that necessary? There's probably just not much to catch. The ice isn't gonna break, it's been negative twenty for like a fucking month."

She was good at ignoring the bursts of anger that came from me. She just let out a sigh and we continued to inch across the ice, listening carefully for any discouraging sounds. She finally put the car in park once we reached the middle of the lake. I opened the moon roof halfway, balanced the tin of tobacco and papers between us, and we both reclined our seats. We watched the sky in silence and didn't mind when it unleashed large flurries of snow on us.

Awake 65 hours.

We continued rolling one cigarette after another, almost reaching the bottom of the tin. We'd been there hours. I watched the snowflakes through the still partially opened moon roof. The flurries had turned into a peaceful snowfall. Flakes drifted towards us in slow motion, allowing me to focus on each individually. One at a time, they swayed from the sky downward, through the open roof and into the stagnant air we were basking in. One at a time the snowflakes landed, and one at a time, they melted. We stayed like this until sunrise.

Awake 74 hours.

"See you later today." She said, smiling before kissing me on the cheek and pulling away. It was Saturday, which meant I'd sleep until evening, before doing something similar again.

One by One
Portland, OR – Fall 1996

"The ants go marching one by one, hoorah! Hoorah! The ants go marching one by one, hoorah! Hoorah!" I sang along with the rest of my kindergarten class.

Every morning we sit in circles and sing songs that are supposed to help our counting. Usually I don't participate and just pretend, but today I am participating. I hate when we're singing because I can't talk to people. Mrs. Bryer also always makes me sit across from her while we're in sing circle. That way she can watch me.

"...the ants go marching one by one, hoorah! Hoorah!"

Pete was sitting next to Mrs. Bryer. Pete talked a lot too and Mrs. Bryer made him sit next to her. At some point during the song Pete had reached under the table behind him and grabbed a marker from the craft box. I knew he grabbed a marker because I could see ink all over his hand. His head is in his lap. I think he's drawing on his face.

"The little one stops to suck his thumb..."

The ink is getting everywhere, Mrs. Bryer is gonna be mad I thought. Pete lifted his head. The room began to spin. My eyes began to fill with tears. It's not ink on Pete's face. He hadn't grabbed a marker – it was a pair of scissors and he has sliced his face repeatedly. He isn't crying.

He isn't making any noise. He's just looking straight at me. But not at me, it looks like he's looking behind me. I can't see his skin anymore. It's just blood.

"Oh my god!" Mrs. Bryer shrieked. "Come on sweetie. Kids stay put!" Mrs. Bryer picked Pete up and ran out of the classroom. Everyone else starts crying and screaming. A hall monitor runs in.

"Okay kids! You were singing right? What song should we sing next?"

* * *

"K makes a KUH noise!" I exclaimed. My mother had just practiced my letter noises with me last night. I knew the answer.

"Good! Oh look class, Pete is here!" Pete walked through the classroom door with his mother at his side. It had been a week since Pete carved his face like a turkey. His face was now wrapped entirely in gauze. There were holes for his eyes, his mouth, and his nostrils. It wouldn't be the image of Pete cutting his face off that stuck with me, but the aftermath. It's this incident that would lead to a phobia of masks. I became nauseated the first time I watched Silence of the Lambs and saw Hannibal lector wearing a leather mask similar to the gauze one I saw Pete wearing.

"Pete wanted to come and say goodbye to all of you." His mother explained.

* * *

Pete was the first of my friends to just disappear. I can't remember anyone trying to explain it to me, I just remember that he was there, bled all over the floor, and disappeared. He was also my first exposure to insanity. Cutting himself wasn't enough – it had been like he was trying to go deep enough with those scissors to rip himself out of his body.

Dozens of friends over the years seem to have vanished into thin air – even with social media.

* * *

"And they all go marching down, into the ground, to get out of the rain."

Eight Days a Week
Portland, OR – Fall 2014

When you've been up twenty-four hours,
your bones begin to feel hollow. Your eyes start
burning. You might be a little nauseous. You can
become sensitive to light.

* * *

By forty-eight hours you can feel your
heartbeat without trying. It's beating faster than
usual and you start to become irritated at the little
things around you. Your mouth is dry and your
tongue begins to scallop - the tip of it becomes
sore from constantly running it across the backs
of your teeth.

* * *

By seventy-two hours, you completely
lose your ability to keep things in order. You
obsessively make to do lists that don't make
sense. Your reason for staying up in the first
place becomes inevitable as you spend most of
your time focusing on how you can stay awake
longer. You start to fear falling asleep. If you fall
asleep the world might stop.

* * *

By ninety-six hours, the paranoia sets in. People know you've stayed awake for four days and they are judging you. You're sweating now too - around your forehead. You might begin to smell a little sour, even with a shower.

* * *

By one-hundred-twenty hours you forget you haven't slept. You have a day of renewal. You might chronically masturbate... say for 11 hours straight.

* * *

By one-hundred-forty-six hours you have episodes of micro-sleep. You'll fall asleep for a few seconds at a time and jerk awake. You'll lose control of some of your physical abilities: Your muscles spasm and you twitch. You see things out of the corner of your eyes - shadows at first and then people, animals, buildings.

* * *

By the seventh day awake, you will come to consciousness on the bathroom floor, having eaten an entire bottle of toothpaste. At least that's how I found myself. I puked up most of it onto my lap and took a shower. I was convinced that if I fell asleep, I would die. I was starving and had unconsciously grabbed my bottle of toothpaste and eaten it. I'd taken hundreds of milligrams of

Adderall. I had stayed awake in my apartment, working on arts and crafts, ignoring phone calls, and deep cleaning.

* * *

I eventually stayed awake for eight days total - the longest I'd ever gone without sleep. I couldn't recognize myself in the mirror. My reflection began to move on its own, and then it morphed into other people. In fear, I ran to my room, took 2mg of Klonopin, and slept for 34 hours.

I called my mom when I woke up and cried hysterically on the phone to her for an hour and made no sense. It terrified her.

Could I ever stop? Would I die?

I hung up on her and turned my phone off. In the mirror I noticed a blackhead on my nose and tried to pop it. It wouldn't come out. I soaked a washcloth in hot water and soaked my face before trying again. It wouldn't budge. I grabbed a sewing needle and stuck it into the blackhead. It still wouldn't come out. It wasn't a blackhead – it looked like a piece of fabric stuck under my skin, so I kept inserting the needle into it, trying to snag the fabric and rip it out. I dug deeper, and deeper. It kept slipping away from me. I decided to try and grab it with tweezers. I pulled bits of skin off surrounding it and still couldn't dislodge it from my face. I grabbed fingernail clippers and tried to pull it out, and was unsuccessful. When I came to, my face was covered in blood. I couldn't find the fabric anymore. I'd removed a large piece of flesh from the bulb of my nose. I taped gauze to my face, took more Klonopin before sleeping for another twelve hours.

I couldn't leave my apartment for weeks. I looked like Hannibal Lector. The scar tissue makes me nauseas every time I look in the mirror.

7th Grade Groupie
Portland, OR – Summer 2004

You're about to eat something sour and your mouth puckers. Fingernails are hovering over a chalkboard and the hair on your neck stands before the screech begins.

Pavlov labeled this classical conditioning. We develop physiological responses to familiar stimuli. Pouring the coke out with trembling hands, I would later decide, was a physiological response without ever having done it before. My body knew what was coming. The shaking continued while I placed the $20 upon the white mound. I ran the edge of my library card over the bill, turning the mound to a pancake. I used the card's edge again, chopping the pancake into lines. The cocaine began to look like snow – light reflected off the now fluffy powder, creating the slightest sparkle.

Fuck did I do it right? Did I forget something? Damnit. He's gonna know I lied about having done coke.

* * *

When I woke up that morning I decided the band was probably at the Jupiter Hotel – Portland's modern day Hyatt House. After scoping out the hotel for a few hours, I finally spotted the band, but more importantly the member who was the object of my affection. The hard part was over: getting into his hotel room would be easy.

The band was notorious for their on and off stage antics – they loved their drugs. I knew this would be my in. I'd gained the courage to approach his door. I knocked, showed him my baggie of cocaine and that was it. I wasn't scared of the man I'd soon seduce, but the coke terrified me. I'd only smoked pot and drank. I'd never actually done coke.

We were alone in his room. My acts of seduction won him over quickly; soon our two sweaty bodies would collide. Like snails we left saliva trails down one another's stomach. They glistened in the beam of sunlight poking through the blinds. My tongue traced his abs – now tense in ecstasy. I'd never made anyone moan before.

We didn't have sex – just a lot of heavy petting. He didn't seem very interested in me – but was more interested in the drugs I had. I was relieved – I'd never been naked in front of anyone before and suddenly I was filled with insecurities I didn't know I had.

We laid half-naked, sniffing coke in his room after we were done rolling around. He'd taken my baggie and I watched as he poured it out on the nightstand and chopped it into lines. I tried to memorize the process of how it was done – there was a card, a bill, chopping, and snorting. I didn't know what a normal amount to do was, so I just did whatever he gave me. He asked if I had a ticket for the show, and when I said no, he said that was fine, that I should tag along with him.

"How old are you?" He finally asked as he zipped his pants.

I told him what he wanted to hear, "eighteen."

* * *

We had done all of the coke I brought. I'd only gotten a gram from my friend's older brother. There was more at the venue – a lot more. While the band was getting ready in the dressing room, he handed me a baggie and asked me to cut some lines for them before they went on. I was honored, but terrified I would do it incorrectly.

In that moment, I felt as though my life had finally begun.

The Boy on the Milk Carton
Minneapolis, MN – January 2013

"Which would you prefer to be on? We will start you on the lowest dose and gradually move up as needed. It will control your mania and we'll keep you on the Xanax to control the panic."

I sat debating if this was what I wanted to do, if this was what I needed. I had changed psychiatrists. After my suicide attempt I had been pumped full of a cocktail of every 1st, 2nd and 3rd line psychiatric medication. None worked. The new psychiatrist looked at me like she pitied me. I wanted to be the boy on the side of the milk carton – gone. Missing. Disappeared. She had informed me of two drugs, Lithium and Lamictal. She told me she had her opinions of both, but said that I was an intelligent boy and that she trusted me to do my research and decide which one I would prefer to try. She said I could call her if I had any questions.

I didn't know much about either drug, but was told that they might help calm my mood swings and my urges to spend money and have sex. All I knew about either was what I had learned from Nirvana and clearly it didn't do wonders for Kurt,

"*...and today I found my friends, in my head.*"

Neither drug sounded ideal, but I was

willing to go to any length to get better. I decided on Lithium.

None of my previous doctors had mentioned Bipolar disorder, but now it was being discussed alongside Bipolar II, and Cyclothymia. No one would however give me a concrete diagnosis. No one would give me a lot of information either. I was basically given a prescription pad and told to figure it out.

When the Skin's Unzipped
Portland, OR – Summer 2015

"I don't think I've felt emotion since I was a little boy."

He shifted onto his side, his now flaccid and suddenly repulsive dick flopping over with the rest of his body.

"What do you mean you don't feel? You just had an orgasm." He offered a smile, an attempt to lend comfort. I hated this. When people want to understand depression but avoid direct questioning by fronting their inquiry with humor.

"An orgasm is a brief moment of physical stimulation - they do nothing for me emotionally. It's just all physical now. At most a moment of relief for this dread. You don't think about suicide, do you? I remember reading The Bell Jar and having the realization that everyone I've known to commit suicide is like the protagonist Esther – they're not always sad, they are more dissatisfied than anything."

* * *

What would he have said back had I said, 'yes, I'm suicidal.' Would he have told me? This was what entered my mind. This is the question that's continued to plague me. Not 'why?' not 'could I have stopped him?' Or the popular, 'were there signs?' The question remains, what the fuck would he have said had I just told him yes? Would he have told me he was suicidal too? Would he have told me that one day soon he would be committing suicide? Would he explain the irony of protesting for a ban on guns to ultimately put a bullet in his own head? Had he even shot one before now?

I didn't focus on the wound but the debris that came from it. The stuff that used to be him but was now compost.

Fuck. I thought, the movies really overdo the gore.

I observed the splatter on the wall and couldn't help but notice the resemblance between it and a Picasso or a Jackson Pollock. It looked like a painting. If he wasn't dead, he could probably profit off of it.

* * *

"No I'm not suicidal. I wish. That'd make all of this too easy. It's like suicide wouldn't be enough because I would die before I got any satisfaction from the killing. Like I cut myself and it does nothing. So I make a slit through one wrist. I tear the flesh. I don't care about the blood or pain. Instead I focus on my skin flapping open, like I'm unzipping a jacket. Like I'm finally removing these binding clothes I was born in, but it's still not enough. So I could slit both wrists but that wouldn't do it either. For it to be enough, I'd need to take that razor and not just slit both wrists but dig that razor in so deep that I don't just break the vein, but I go under the vein, and rip the entire thing out, on both wrists. I keep thinking about this and I think at this point, it's the only way I could feel again and even then, it'd only be for a moment. It's really upsetting because I'd go unconscious from blood loss long before I could get that moment. I will forever be that fat kid chasing the goddamn ice cream truck. I will never experience the satisfaction that I yearn. It doesn't matter how many therapists I see, or how many medications I'm put on. None of it will ever be enough. I'm trapped."

* * *

I can't breathe.
You're not panicking.
You're not panicking.
This isn't a panic attack.
Why can't I breathe?
This isn't out of shock.
All of the oxygen has been sucked from the room.
That's it.
The oxygen is gone but I'm fine.
Where'd he go?
I was looking straight at him.
Now all I see is the ceiling.

I try and brace myself, I use my left hand to try and close the door behind me and my body takes over, stumbling back. I hear it click shut finally. The oxygen is slowly coming back and I slide carefully down the door until I'm sure I've reached the floor. Logic has crept back into me. I realize I'm on the floor. Sitting isn't making me feel better – I still feel like someone is spinning me.

Stability doesn't exist, nothing is sturdy in a world that always rotates.

It's become impossible for me to stand.

I'm stuck on the goddamn floor and I can't see him.

I clench my fists. I clench my jaw. I clench my ass - anything to make this fucking room stop spinning for one second.

This isn't real. I've finally lost it. I've crossed that threshold between our world and the one they say doesn't exist. I'm fucking insane but if I'm insane, that means you're still here. You're going to push open this door I'm slouched against any second. None of this is really happening. I know the room isn't really spinning. And I know that when I unclench my fists, the rest of my body and finally my eyes, your body won't be here. That wall behind your couch will still be spotless and white. The left side of your perfect face will still be there. You won't have left me here in hell, forever alone to singe in these lakes of fire.

* * *

He stared at me, scrunching his forehead. His brows moved toward one another. I felt like he was memorizing my face – as if in that second he had used a mental camera to photograph me in my most primitive state. He rolled over and turned the lamp off before facing me again to pull me in tight. He kissed my head but his lips remained pressed tightly to my skull.

He let out a deep breath before saying, "Don't worry, one day you'll no longer be that fat kid and you'll catch up to that ice cream truck."

Boy Troubles
Portland, OR – December 2014

You get sick a lot. Weird viruses, bacterial infections, fungal growths... the drugs make you not care so much, but the combination of sleep deprivation, using, and promiscuous sex can take a toll on your body. However, you will refuse to correlate those things, no matter how obvious they may be. You might find yourself standing before the toilet, with the need to urinate, but no urine coming out – at least that's what happened to me.

I tried turning on the water – nothing. I tried sitting down on the toilet and relaxing – nothing. I tried sticking one hand in warm water – nothing. My bladder at this point was starting to cramp. When I thought I was going to lose it, I went to the emergency room.

* * *

I made a grand entrance, screaming "my bladder is gonna pop! Open me up!" As I ran past the front desk and tried to barge into the triage station. I was stopped by a nurse before collapsing on the floor, on the verge of tears saying "my bladder hurts, I have to pee and it won't come out. Please, it's gonna burst or something. I need emergency surgery."

Despite my frequent visits to the emergency room, they didn't argue with me. A nurse took me back to a bed without getting any identification yet. A technician met us in the room with an ultrasound and held it to my pelvis while I gave the nurse my ID.

"He's full, we need a catheter right away."

A what? I thought. Oh Jesus. I was terrified but the pain was too great. My bladder was on the verge of rupturing - it was the only time I'd ever seen a nurse move with urgency in front of a patient.

I can't remember who pulled my pants down but I was squirming from the pain while they did it, like an infant getting their diaper changed. I pictured the scene in Alien where the baby alien rips its way through the torso. My bladder was about to announce itself to the room. One man came in - a doctor or nurse, who knows - and held me down because I was starting to flail.

"You'll feel a slight pinch." The nurse said as she grabbed the head of my penis. Another cliché: I saw stars. A rumbling came up through my body, into my throat where it felt like a rock was lodged, and out my mouth. I screamed like I have never screamed in my life and instinctively took a swing at the man holding me down.

"It won't go in." The nurse sounded alarmed.

I felt like I was having an out of body experience. I felt detached from reality except for the pain that kept me grounded.

If it wouldn't go in, what was the pain from?

I tried to pay attention to what they were saying. It was something about internal swelling and the tube not being able to make it all the way to the bladder. There was a blockage of sorts.

"Here, switch with me." The man I'd tried to throat-punch switched with the nurse.

Within second the stars were back. My body lifted from the bed and slammed back into it, I began kicking my legs and kicked the man in the stomach and then the chest. I couldn't help it - I knew it wasn't his fault but the pain was unbearable. I was screaming uncontrollably now. The pressure in my bladder was gone but it felt like someone had severed my shaft in half. Every muscle in my body eventually gave and I collapsed, whimpering and crying. Snot and tears coated my face as I tried to bury it in the pillow. I was trembling now. It was freezing but I was drenched in sweat. I tried to open my eyes but couldn't see straight.

"I'm sorry for hitting and swearing." I gasped. "I've never hurt this bad before. It won't stop."

Someone came in and gave me painkillers and benzos. Slowly machines were being hooked up for my vitals and an IV.

They gave me some time and turned off the lights before coming back in to get my medical history, and other information.

The pain wouldn't stop. I couldn't bring myself to look down but pictured my penis cut in half while I bled to death

.

* * *

I'd been there hours while tests were run. No one could quite figure out what was wrong with me. They said my prostate was inflamed. They treated me like I had an STI - giving me a shot of ceftriaxone and a Z-pack.

I was discharged with no answers and told to come back in a few days to have the catheter removed.

* * *

I mostly sat in the dark, unable to look at myself. I didn't change or bathe. The catheter was attached to a bag that tied to my ankle. Every few hours I had to drain it. I tried not to drink anything because I didn't want to acknowledge that I was hooked to a tube that went inside my genitals.

I hobbled around. If I took a step too big it would tug on the tube and a dull pain would thud deep in my pelvis. I was too embarrassed for anyone to know and hid that week. When a few days had passed and I could have the catheter removed, I took a cab to the hospital. My thick greasy hair hung over my eyes. I could smell my BO. I was still wearing the same clothes. When the nurse came in, a man I didn't recognize - as chipper as ever - I pictured myself ripping his throat out with my teeth.

I undressed and put on a beautiful fluorescent hospital gown. The man said "okay let's get this thing out" and sat down, sliding toward my legs.

"What are you doing?" I demanded.

"Taking the catheter out." He said inquisitively.

"No you're not. That was the worst pain I've ever felt. Get an anesthesiologist in here to put me to sleep before you touch it."

"We don't put people to sleep for this. It doesn't hurt coming out. I promise."

He looked sincere, but I warned him "just ask the other nurses. I start throwing punches when I see stars."

I laid back, and put the pillow over my face - biting it.

The pain was worse this time. It felt like someone took my stomach and pulled it through my urethra. I kicked the nurse as hard as I could in the forehead - again, an accident. The nurse fell backwards and off his chair as he called for help.

Again, I was surrounded by emergency department staff. I was in too much pain to really know what was going on. I wouldn't quit flailing around like a slug that had salt poured on it. My body swung back and forth. I was slamming into the railing on the hospital bed. I don't know what happened to the nurse I kicked over. I heard someone call out "you didn't deflate the balloon."

The balloon is what prevents the catheter from coming out on its own. The guy didn't deflate it, so when he yanked on the tube, it did indeed pull my intestines towards my urethra. I didn't feel bad about kicking him anymore.

I negotiated and pleaded with the doctor and nurses. I wanted to be sedated. I wanted anything other than being conscious when they tried to take it out again. They tried to meet me halfway and gave me more Ativan and some morphine this time. That wasn't halfway at all. I wanted them to knock me out.

Two nurses came and held both of my hands at my request. I positioned my body like I was giving birth. The nurse this time (a new one, a woman) said she was gonna pull on three. I knew she would pull on two. When she did she jumped back, dodging my foot heading for her face. I screamed every swear word I could think of, but curled up much quicker into a ball this time. Sobbing hysterically.

I went home that night and inspected my penis. It looked the same but I was scared to touch it. A friend had picked me up from the hospital that night and we sat in my living room snorting oxy I had leftover. I got off the floor to use the bathroom. I stood before the toilet. Nothing came out. I turned on the water. Nothing came out. I listened to sounds of the ocean and waterfalls on my phone. Nothing came out.

I collapsed on the floor crying. All I wanted was to pee. My friend came in and asked what was wrong. I told him everything. He picked me up and carried me to his car, where he drove me to the emergency room. I stumbled in, moving like a zombie in my sorrow.

Back on the hospital bed I pleaded with the nurse to just let my bladder burst. She said that would be worse. I didn't care. I cried hysterically and said I'd rather have surgery. I refused to let her touch me.

She left the room for a few minutes before coming back in with painkillers and Ativan.

Once the meds kicked in, I laid back and inhaled deeply. Feeling like I was a cloud, I giggled a little but was still nervous. Lightning and thunder came to my cloud when they inserted the catheter. I cried and hyperventilated again, too tired to swear. They left me in the dark again.

I refused to leave until I had answers. They couldn't figure out what was wrong with me. Eventually a doctor said he thought it was prostatitis. He said I needed a course of antibiotics. I asked why the first round didn't work. He said the wall of the prostate is thick and it takes a lot of antibiotics for a long period of time to penetrate it. He said I would have to leave the catheter in for ten days.

I was supposed to head to Minneapolis for a few days for the holidays.

* * *

When I went through airport security, I whispered to TSA that I had a medical device under my clothing. They nodded but didn't pass along the message to the person doing the X-ray. They hassled me about it and finally I screamed "I have a catheter!"

The man let me through with no more questions asked.

* * *

I bowled a 78 with a catheter. I was proud of myself. I left the floor to go to the bathroom and empty the catheter into the urinal. When I came out my friends were packing up and ready to leave. I hugged them goodbye and left.

When I went outside, my car was gone. In disbelief I walked for blocks, thinking maybe I'd parked somewhere else. I'd still been binging on benzos and oxy so I didn't mind much at first and even laughed at the situation. I called the local towing company. They had my car. My phone was about to die and when I tried to call a cab, it powered off. I asked someone on the street to look up the address of the towing company for me and took off in that direction on foot. I walked for over an hour in subzero temperatures. Chewing another Ativan every few blocks - they were only half milligrams. When I reached the tow place, I stood at the edge of the parking lot. My bladder felt full. I had to empty my catheter. I reached down and pretended to tie my shoelaces. I slid the latch on my catheter bag. Nothing came out. I pulled up my pant leg and was in complete disbelief: the bag full of urine had frozen. Not just the bag but the tube.

The sign on the door of the towing place had a "back in 15 minutes sign." As I stood outside waiting, the tube continued to freeze higher and higher up, before the top at the entrance of my penis froze. It felt like icicles penetrating my dick.

When they returned, I ran in, said my car had been towed, but I had to use the bathroom.

They pointed me in the direction of the restroom. Once inside, I took off my pants, despite it being a community bathroom, and put my leg in the sink and ran hot water over it. I unlatched the catheter so that as it thawed, it would drain out into the sink.

A man who worked for the towing company came in after half of the bag had slushed out. He started screaming at me and threatened to call the police. Others ran in. I took my leg out of the sink and remained calm and tried to explain it to him. I grabbed my pants and got dressed in a hurry. I explained to them that it was basically their fault. They felt enough sympathy for me that they let me go with my car and without calling the police.

I was too high to drive home. I found a secluded place to park and decided to sleep for a few hours. In my rush to get dressed, I must have broken the partially frozen tube from its attachment to the bag, because after having driven a few blocks I realized my shoe was full of urine.

* * *

I went to a hospital in Minnesota to have the catheter removed before flying back to Portland. It didn't hurt this time - the blockage/swelling must have been gone. This doctor couldn't tell me for sure why my body had done this either. When pressed, he said it could've been something sexually related and advocated abstinence. He asked if I used drugs and warned of them compromising my immune system. Unfortunately, at the time I learned nothing from this and carried on as usual.

All Things Know
Chicago, IL – Summer 2012

The first time I met her reminded me of the first time I listened to Judee Sill – I felt so alive. She resembled a Q-Tip; she had a tall, slender frame, with big blonde hair. She had turned herself into an art project. Her lightly bronzed skin was largely covered in tattoos. Her smile – often shown during times of mischief – bore a golden tooth. Even her slender figure had been altered by two large balls of silicone that were strategically implanted in her chest. She was perfect.

* * *

It was 103 degrees out, and I was hauling ass through Wisconsin on Highway 94. I listened to Sufjan Stevens the entire way. I had dropped everything and left Minneapolis, heading straight for Chicago. I switched back and forth between having the air conditioning on and the windows down as I tried to remember the last time I saw her, but I couldn't. She had invited to me to stay with her in Chicago before I would make my return back to school. She's one of the few people I would take off work, and drive across the Midwest for. She wasn't just that person for me, but I think she was that person for everyone who knew her. I started to think about that time at the lake when she asked a kid for a lighter, and he only had matches. She used his match, and after he walked what had to have been several blocks to his car just to get a lighter in case she needed it again.

* * *

I try and think of all of her tattoo's and the only ones that come to me vividly are the rosary that hangs down her chest and the word empathy in big bold letters across her back that represents her sobriety – we met in a twelve-step program. She'd had thousands of dollars in tattoos but she had never paid for any of them. People were often more than willing to give instead of charging. They wanted their art on her body: The perfect canvas.

* * *

We went out for frozen yogurt late that night to try and escape the sweltering heat wave that was terrorizing those stuck in the city. She had a thing with John Cusack and he showed up on a moped with a friend. Despite it being 100 degrees, he wore sweatpants and a hoodie, with a bandana on. He looked like Tom Hanks in Castaway. I was unimpressed. Next to her anyone was unimpressive. I'm sure he felt the same way about me – he barely shook my hand. I mostly focused on her and how she interacted with him. He was watching her as closely as I was.

When he rode off into the night on his moped, we returned to her place. We both talked a lot about addiction, and our sanity and insanity. We talked about how we brought people into our lives and ultimately just ended up tormenting them. She told me it wasn't that we were trying to hurt people, or make their lives bad, but that we brought them into our worlds because we were trying to make our lives better. We weren't malicious, just selfish. It was inevitable that we would hurt everyone who became close to us.

* * *

On the 4th of July we went to a small town in Indiana and lit off illegal fireworks. The police came. I ran and slid under a car to hide. She was wearing an extra-large men's button up with no pants on and did a curtsy to the police officer. He laughed and continued to drive. She lost it laughing when I rolled out from underneath the car. I have lost track of how many times she's gotten us out of trouble with the police using a curtsy.

* * *

I had relapsed and I heard she had also. We still talked but not as regularly. We would always be close. Time and frequency wouldn't stop that. I was busy checking a friend into the psych ward when she began blowing up my phone. I didn't answer as I was a little busy. She had tried calling me a few times that month, but when I was using, phone calls were too much for me to handle. After not answering this time came a stream of text messages...

"YOUR A HORRIBLE PERSON."

"I AM DONE WITH YOU. YOU NEVER ANSWER YOUR PHONE. You will never see me again. You're such a shitty friend."

I texted back "You're*"

Then I followed it up with "I'm busy checking a friend into the psych ward – maybe you should come and join us and check yourself in."

She sent text messages saying terrible things. I took a photo of the psych waiting room and said "I'm literally checking in someone who threatened to kill themselves and other people. I'm a little busy." She said "I don't care!" She didn't care about anyone outside of herself during these episodes and I didn't either. I blocked her on all social media and then blocked her number. I could tell that she was using again. I was too and that didn't help matters. It didn't matter that we were close. Despite our mutual love, we were indispensable to one another. It was the classic case of two addicts absolutely mad about one another, ultimately causing each other's demise. This happens whenever love and addiction meet: Sid and Nancy, Kurt and Courtney, Jim and Pamela. We kill ourselves and each other. We don't even mean to.

* * *

My friend I was checking in that day got out of the psych ward. I hear he's homeless now, but he's not threatening to kill anyone – some would say that's a success by American standards.

She and I didn't talk for years after that until the funeral of a loved one. We hadn't been trying to ruin each other's lives – we were trying to make our lives better. But we both inevitably got burned. One day we would repair ourselves, and the love would be there still, without the madness.

Cash Cab

New York City, NY – March 2011

The plane descended beneath the clouds and there it was in all of its glory: The Manhattan skyline at night. It was mightier than the words that had been written about it; it was more beautiful than the photos I'd seen of it. I was filled with ease and had the expectation that I would find nirvana under those city lights. I couldn't wait.

I got off the plane and was surprised. I expected more from the airport. I expected there to be thousands of people crammed together like cigarettes in a pack. La Guardia was fairly empty though. I recited the directions from my friend to myself as I walked to the baggage claim. *56 Sutton Place, take the Queensboro Bridge.*

I grabbed my bags and stepped outside into the cool Spring night. I put in my headphones and listened to Simon & Garfunkel's "The Only Living Boy in New York." I sat for a minute smoking a cigarette, trying to contain an excitement I'd never felt. New York was the city dreams were discovered in, it was the city dreams were made in. I'd been sober exactly one year and I was going to figure out who I was and what I was meant to do.

I pretended like I knew what I was doing and walked right up to a cab and told the driver the address and to take the Queensboro Bridge. He put my bag in the trunk and we were off. I watched out the window in awe at all of the buildings we passed. We hadn't even hit Manhattan yet and I knew I was in love.

* * *

I showed up at my friend's apartment, and shook the hands of the door man and then the elevator man. They both looked at me with suspecting eyes. I wasn't on the West Coast or in the Midwest – people don't do that here. After checking my ID, the elevator man took me into the elevator and pressed the button for the floor I needed to go to. He pointed me to the right apartment door and left. Before I could knock, my friend swung the door open and wrapped her arms around me. The apartment was spacious with wood floors, high ceilings, and a balcony overlooking Roosevelt Island. It was the most elegant place I'd ever been in. It felt like a museum. It was fitting for my friend who looked like Audrey Hepburn. We'd met in Florida and she invited me to follow her to NYC. She was perfect – I'd never met anyone with so many conflictions within themselves. She was beautiful but wounded. She was kind but needy. She was smart but apathetic. She wanted to be adored and presented her heart to anyone who would smile.

She opened my suitcase and picked out the clothes I would wear going out that night. Black jeans, black t-shirt, black jacket, black boots – all black everything. I learned my first lesson of *society* that night: older women exit the elevator first, then younger women, then older men, then younger men.

I can't remember if we went to Marquee that night or Juliette's. I just remember a half-naked woman playing an electric violin along with the DJ's music. I stared at her with my jaw dropped – no one else paid any attention. That morning when we left the club, I snapped a picture as the sun was rising over Manhattan, blocked by the buildings, and making patterns of light through the grid of the city.

* * *

We sat at Flip – the restaurant inside Bloomingdales – eating. I watched her closely and observed the correct utensils to use. We'd already been to Bergdorf Goodman and Barneys that day. We talked about art, philosophy, religion, and politics. She challenged me and pushed me. With her help I was blending into this society that I was never meant to fit into.

We would spend evenings lounging in her bed, listening to music, until it was time to go out. Usually around ten or eleven. I tried to mimic her. She annunciated her words. She chose them carefully. She was poise. She was a Manhattan debutante – but without the ruffles. She would befriend anyone. *Kindness is endearing.*

We went to a club that night in the Meatpacking District called Kiss & Fly. A friend from Rhode Island joined us. We danced and talked and mingled. I fit in. No one I met knew I wasn't from there and that I didn't belong. The kids making fun of others waiting outside the club, people they referred to as "bridge and tunnel people" never pointed their fingers at me. I realized on the dance floor that night that I was a chameleon. Doors that had always been closed to me would open if I could just blend in.

We left that night in a cab while my friend from Rhode Island drunkenly yelled at those we drove by that we were in Cash Cab (a reality show about winning money playing trivia in a cab). People cheered us on. I don't remember who was laughing harder, me or the cab driver. I felt the most alive I'd ever felt since getting sober. I could laugh again.

That week we browsed the Met, the MoMA, the Whitney, and the Guggenheim. She taught me about art. She taught me how to talk about art. She taught me how to appreciate art. I wanted it all; I wanted to be her.

When I would finally leave Manhattan I would dedicate myself to doing it all. I wanted to read all of the books, learn all of the languages, study art, philosophy, sociology, anthropology, biology, feminism and diplomacy. I wanted to sit in some café in Brooklyn and write things that people would want to read.

My friend believed in me. She created a fork in the road I was on. One path led back to drugs and apathy, but with it, the diminishment of everything that caused me pain: anxiety about life and death, the world around us, and expectations.

The other path is one she showed me I was capable of walking. It was a path of creativity and academia. It was a path of self-discovery. It was a path of professionalism and big dreams, but with all of that came pain, and fear of failure. It was confrontation. It was everything I'd spent my entire life avoiding. The pressure was enough to make me lose it and become some sad statistic.

New York created an ambivalence in me. Drugs or sobriety. Sanity or insanity. Responsibility or recklessness. Happiness and pain or numbness and decay. I had options. If only I could make a choice.

All That's Left is Ash
Minneapolis, MN – February 2013

It's a little past midnight and you're driving home. Your eyes are tired - the radio is giving you what little energy you have. A deer runs in front of your car and you slam on your brakes.

As you walk your dog down the street you pass a funeral home and see two men carrying a coffin towards the hearse – it's only four feet long.

The first time you saw footage of people leaping out of the twin towers as planes impaled the concrete walls, sending the buildings towards the ground.

This is panic disorder – these moments. The only difference is your mind continues to linger. The deer will run off and you will be asleep soon. You will forget about the dead child. Your mind will leave 9/11 and move onto the next national disaster. Panic is constant. Your heart will continue to skip a beat; your mind will race. Your life will be fear and dread. This was something I had to come to terms with. It wasn't just going to pass. It wasn't a bad dream, it wasn't just another life hurdle: it was a new life, one I didn't get to choose.

I'd been in therapy for months and on an array of medications and I wasn't any better. I was better at coping, and being in public, but I didn't feel any better. I appeared to be functioning like those around me, but the pain inside never subsided. If anything it got worse as I grappled with thoughts of *will I be like this the rest of my life?*

Lady Godiva
Minneapolis, MN – September 2007

The girl from Chicago had a sister I became close with. That song Bette Davis Eyes always reminded me of her. Her hair really was Harlow gold, she had these perfect lips and pure skin. The first time I met her, her teal dress flowing as she approached me, she put her headphones on me and said "this is the anthem of my life." It was called "Snake Charmer" by Bassnectar. Dubstep hadn't gotten big in the US yet but she knew all about it. She knew all about everything. I knew in that moment that I loved her boldly and I didn't even know her name yet. I didn't have to think twice and never looked back. Every person to meet her fell in love. But none of them could ever have her. No one could. There's that quote from Breakfast at Tiffany's "But you can't give your heart to a wild thing: the more you do, the stronger they get. Until they're strong enough to fly away." I'd never met anyone like her. She was the real life Holly Golightly and everyone wanted something from her: their attention, a date, her friendship - I just wanted to be in the same room as her.

* * *

We had classes together that Fall and she was brilliant too. Every teacher underestimated her on the first day, but never after that. She never had to try. Her effort was flawless.

* * *

She was the DJ at my 16th birthday party. She never drank or did drugs like everyone else. She also never made a big deal about it. It just wasn't "her thing." She was too cool. She didn't need drugs to be exciting. "I am drugs" she once said. Someone said the cops were outside that night. I've never seen someone run as fast as she did in stilettos. It was one of her many talents.

* * *

She was the most beautiful girl in our school but she didn't seem to notice. She was popular but she didn't want it. She was smart but she didn't care about impressing anyone. She always called me over to sit with her at lunch. I was surprised and honored every time. She was sitting with a weird art kid one day. She said "this is Cam, he's cool." She didn't care that Cam actually wasn't cool and didn't have many friends. She was his friend. She would be friends with anyone. She was kind. She had a way of taking the underdog under her wing.

* * *

I was going to go out on St. Patrick's Day and do as many drugs as possible. Instead, she asked me to hangout. We laid in bed and listened to The Fugees. She taught me about A Tribe Called Quest and hip hop. We talked about our favorite diseases and serial killers. We formed a friendship that night outside of everyone else. I hadn't known it at the time but she would remain one of my best friends.

* * *

"You're fucking up. Don't be fucking stupid." She said to me.

It was our senior year and I was spending my lunches snorting coke and pain pills.

"You've got something going for you that no one else does. You're real. You're supposed to write about all of the pretenders and you can't do that if you're dead."

* * *

A few months later I would get sober. In my adjustment period she would come and sit with me in my room and listen to music. She never made a big deal about it or anything. She just said "drugs are stupid. I watched my sister kill herself for years before she got sober. Get sober this once and stick with it." She told me I should talk to her sister.

* * *

When we graduated high school, she and

I stood at the edge of the auditorium before the ceremony. We laughed at the girls moving to Hollywood to be actresses, and those moving to Miami to be models. We guessed which jocks would get beer bellies and DUI's by 21 (most of our guesses ended up being accurate). We placed bets on which people would go to college only to give up their career for a kid, spouse, and picket fence. She was going to be a doctor, and I was going to be a writer.

* * *

I'd moved back to Portland to be a writer. We kept in touch and anytime I went to Minneapolis, she was one of the first people I saw. I flew back to stay for an entire summer. I went to her house; she was living with her sister who I had become friends with. She started drinking – sort of. She would have a glass of whatever at a party, and would casually sip on the same glass all night. We went out that night, she drank but didn't get drunk. I'm not sure I ever saw her actually drunk. She liked control, she liked sensibility, she liked having composure. Every man that night was watching her. She didn't pay attention. She had a man, but he was enlisted and was somewhere down south. We hid in the bathroom at the party, locked the door, and sat on this stranger's floor talking until enough angry people outside of the door piled up. I thought she was the happiest person I knew, and the only one to have it all figured out. She knew what she wanted.

* * *

I went back to Minneapolis again that December. She had dropped out of school "temporarily," and had started stripping. Her boyfriend was still at the base. She didn't need the money… she chose to strip. I always wondered why but never asked. That wasn't what our friendship was about. We didn't question each other. We just accepted. Enough people were already judging her, I didn't need to be another bridge burned. She'd also said she was doing coke and taking Xanax. I told her to be careful, and she assured me it was casual.

* * *

She became a flip book. The pages were turning quickly and with it, her image. It was altering faster and faster and was impossible to keep up with. Her change was faster than anything I'd ever experienced. When I returned to Minnesota, she would be awake for days at a time and then would sleep for 16-20 hours. I finally broke down and expressed concern. She said "I just need to do my thing right now." I never understood why she felt compelled to do these things though. Where had the sudden change come from? She had always stayed away from the things she was now doing. She was dating a guy who worked at the strip club. I heard rumors that he had ties to organized crime. Her sister and I took turns staking him out. Her family had a holiday party, and I ran into her as I walked over... she was parked down the road, snorting coke in her car. I told a mutual friend of ours once she and I got to the party. What followed was a half-assed, accusatory intervention. I didn't participate. That wasn't how I wanted things to play out. I knew she would be angry and feel attacked. She fled the party. When I saw her again we talked about it. She wasn't mad at me for my part in it, she was mad at how it was handled. She assured me she had control over the problem.

* * *

I was away for a couple of years this time. While I was gone she ended up in prison for drug charges. She had started doing heroin. A friend of ours found her nodding out in a car on the side of the road once. The last time I saw her was by accident. I was on a quick trip to the Twin Cities when I came out of a gas station and she yelled at me from a car in the parking lot. I ran over and hugged her tightly. After we embraced, she asked if I would like to smoke a cigarette with her in her car. Her car was full of blankets, pillows, clothes, etc. She had been living in and out of it. She had heroin in her cup holder and put it in the glovebox when I got in. I ignored it. After we caught up and talked for a bit I told her I had to go. She didn't want me to, so I stayed a little while longer. When we did finally part ways, I grabbed her hand and told her I would always be there for her and she could call me anytime. We hugged and parted ways.

* * *

We kept tabs on each other over the years. We hadn't talked in a couple of months when one night she began persistently messaging me. I left a date early so that I could talk to her, because it was random and insistent, I worried something might be wrong. Nothing was wrong. Our conversation went like this:

Her: Hey

Me: How are you? I was thinking about you recently!

Her: Same. Not great, life is complicated and hard sometimes. But what's new. How about you?

Me: I'm good, just busy lately. Are you back at your mom's place?

Her: No. Just for tonight and the holiday I guess.

Me: Are you in Minneapolis then?

Her: Yes

Me: Okay well that's good. At least you're close to home. Are you living somewhere that's safe and secure?

Her: Oh not at all. I still live over in North. And I don't have a secure place to live but me and my boyfriend have a few houses over there. I won't stay there if I'm alone and he's in jail right now.

Only god knows what happens before we show up or after we leave… so I try to be scarce.
Me: Well I'm worried about you. How long is he in jail for? Try to have a good holiday.
Her: He could go to prison but I hope not. Yeah I suppose.

We also talked about Santeria, the Pacific Northwest, and she asked me if I'd met Kurt Cobain's ghost yet. I told her no but I'd been to the house he died in. She asked how it was and I told her it was beautiful but really sad.

Within forty-eight hours her mom would reach out to me and tell me she had died. I'll never know if she knew deep down that she would be dying soon, and if that's why she reached out. The day she died I had been writing in my journal about her. Within hours of writing the last sentence, she died. Part of me died with her that day. I never got to help save her the same way she helped save me. I don't think she wanted to be saved. I think the world had broken her. I think she realized what a truly horrible place it could be and she began to run from it as fast as she could.

* * *

I returned to Minneapolis for the funeral. I held it together well until I saw her sister who I hadn't talked to in years. She was different now – she was raising a toddler, she no longer had a fling with John Cusack. She had driven in from Chicago. We hadn't talked since a fight we'd had years earlier while I was checking a friend into a psych-ward. We embraced for a long time. With anyone else, the friendship probably wouldn't have been salvaged, but from a fellow addict and basket-case... we understood each other, and the apology our arms said as they wrapped around each other was enough.

* * *

I got in a cab to head home and Bette Davis Eyes started playing on the radio. I started to laugh. I took it as a sign that she was with me. Like Holly Golightly, we all gave her our heart and she flew away. I had never wanted anything in return for the love I gave, I just wanted to be around her, and for some time, I got what I wanted.

Mom Panties

Fort Lauderdale, FL – November 2010

I was nineteen. He was thirty-six. He'd just been made partner at a successful law firm in South Florida. When you're nineteen and they say they love you, you believe them. When you're nineteen, you believe they're loyal to you, even when their good looks, Porsche, and wandering eyes make you nervous. I'd never been in a real relationship.

We met online, like every other millennial couple. Well I was a millennial – he wasn't. He would pick me up from campus, but would never actually enter the campus. He would park down the road and make me walk to his car. He said it was embarrassing to be picking someone up from a campus. When he would drop me off, he would also drop me at the end of the road, or make me take a cab. He lived in Fort Lauderdale, but we only ever went out in Delray Beach or West Palm Beach – he didn't want to run into anyone he knew. At nineteen you accept these things, and don't read into them.

I did meet a partner in his law firm, and his brother. I eventually met a couple of his friends. I was always referred to as a "friend." At nineteen, this is normal, or you tell yourself it is. I was self-conscious and didn't like taking nude photos, but he would guilt trip me into sending them. One night at dinner when I finally told him I didn't feel comfortable doing this, he left the restaurant, leaving me with a bill he knew I couldn't afford. It had been celebrating my birthday. I over-drafted my card for dinner that night. He was waiting outside to get the last word in, and made me take a cab back to Boca. I didn't have money for it, and a friend had to meet me to pay the driver. I stayed. At nineteen you tell yourself it's normal for couples to fight.

When I decided to surprise him one Sunday at his apartment, he was with someone else. He made me wait outside until they were done. He told me he had "too much love to give just one person." I asked "does your love come with chlamydia or are you being safe?" He shut the door on me.

This went on through Halloween, and Thanksgiving. I decided to reciprocate his toxicity and looked through his phone when he was in the shower one night. It wasn't just the one other guy, but a different one every night I wasn't at his place. I left before he got out of the shower. When he texted me I said "I have diarrhea and had to leave." On my way home that night I texted my friend and asked her "do you have any large, old panties I can have? No questions asked." She gave me three pairs.

I told myself I would never allow myself to stay in a toxic relationship. I also wouldn't be made a fool of. I'd been sober about seven months but this part of me lingered, a part of me where I allowed resentment and maliciousness to flourish. In retrospect, I believe these were early

signs of my upcoming mental illness. I had traits
that psychiatrists would call "borderline."

I took the panties my friend gave me to
his apartment the next time I went over. When he
was in the shower, I laid them out on the bed and
took photos. I got his brother's number off his
phone, as well as the partner at his law firm that
I'd met. I left before he got out of the shower,
taking the panties with me. I didn't want to leave
any evidence.

I texted his partner at the law firm and
said "I don't know who else to turn to. Out of
everyone in Justin's life, I've met you the most.
He has all of these nude photos on his computer
with questionable legality, as the people look
very young. Just trying to look out for you and
the law firm. I think he needs help."

I texted his brother next. A brother who
was a hardcore conservative with a history of not
being okay with his brother's sexuality. I sent
him the photos of the panties and said "I'm
worried about your brother. Since he was a kid he
has been stealing your mother's underwear. He is
always trying to get me to wear them. He told me
he also used to steal your underwear. I can't do it
anymore, so I'm leaving him. He needs help."

I blocked his number, blocked the
numbers I had just texted, and blocked him and
everyone he knew on social media by the time I
made it back to campus that night. Some friend's
thought I had taken it too far, some thought it was
hilarious. I thought nothing of it and moved on,
beginning a trend in which I was okay with

retaliating against people who had wronged me, feeling no remorse.

The Elephant Man
San Diego, CA – April 2016

"I have Proteus syndrome - like the elephant man."

I had a sick fascination of disease and disorder and even I was unaware of what that was.

"I don't know what that is."

"You've never seen Elephant Man? It's a really good movie."

"OK but that still doesn't tell me what it is you have."

"Look," he said, "feel here." He had me press down on his left cheek. There was a bone on top of his cheekbone - one that wasn't supposed to be there. I asked him what it was.

He said "it's a growth. Your body starts to mutate. "See?" He stuck out his tongue. Near the backside of his tongue appeared the beginning of a second tongue.

He told me there's less than 200 people worldwide with the disease and there's really nothing you can do about it. He wasn't worried. He said it didn't bother him and it kind of fascinated him. I asked if it would kill him and he said he didn't know. We talked more about it for a while before I felt obligated to confide in him what I'd been holding in – that I have Huntington's Disease.

I told him. He laughed and asked why I made such a big deal about it. For days I'd been telling him there was something I wanted to talk to him about. I told him about my ex and how I'd been dumped when he found out that I had Huntington's. We had bonded over our love of science, only to discover we both were products of faulty genetics. It became something Gothic – we were drawn to each other in illness. The scent of death was on us, and it was intoxicating. For me, it had created a morbid bond that no one else would be able to understand. A bond in which both lovers would ultimately die. It was like Romeo and Juliet, but instead of dying from poison and a knife through the heart, we would die at the hands of disease and disorder.

* * *

We'd sit at Blacks Beach in San Diego late at night - after the crowds had left - and would hold one another. He'd stare at the sky until I became jealous of it. He'd point to various stars and tell me about astronomy, while I'd tell him about astrology.

* * *

I took him to Los Angeles. He'd never been.
"You're like a movie star. It's crazy here!" He'd said. It was the biggest city he'd ever been to. As we walked the city I pointed out my personal landmarks, as well as historical ones.

"I od'd here once." I pointed to a restaurant.

"Here's the house I stayed in one Summer." I showed him the home in Laurel Canyon where I'd spent my nights sniffing coke with boys playing guitars.

By the end of our trip he'd begun to yearn to try drugs, go to these parties, meet more people; he'd never had an interest in any of that before me. On our drive back to San Diego, I worried to myself that he wanted to live my history - something I'd left in the past for a reason. He was young, nineteen. I was twenty-four and had already done the things he'd yet experienced.

* * *

At some point while we were dating, I'd started taking Adderall again. I'd gone from being sober for years to taking 30mg extended release pills alongside two 20mg immediate release pills – an absurd amount. It was easy for a white college educated guy to get some SoCal doctor to prescribe him a handful of amphetamines. I binged and would stay awake for days – fixated on writing, the 2016 presidential election, and weird art projects I decided to start while tweaking out at 4am.

* * *

"You cheated on me!" I'd texted him. I knew he hadn't cheated on me, but I'd cheated on him. So I needed to gaslight him. I'd been completely spun out and had dived into some serious psychosis, and had gone on a sex binge with strangers in Hillcrest. I wanted him to cheat on me so I wouldn't feel guilty. He was pissed I'd accused him of it, and dumped me over a text message.

"I can't do this anymore. You're losing it."

"Are you dumping me over a text message?"

"I guess I am. I'm sorry."

"I love you."

"You don't love me."

But I did. He's the only person I'd ever been in love with, and the pain from him ending our relationship was severe. I felt like I was dying. I wanted him to hurt.

"You're going to continue to mutate until your outside is as ugly as your inside, and no one will ever love you again because no one will be able to look at you, and you'll die alone."

That was the last thing I ever said to him. He blocked my number after that. I'd ruined the most honest relationship I'd had. I'm still unsure if it was unintentional, subconsciously intentional, or if the drugs had just made me crazy – or if at my very core I'm just crazy, and capable of being that cruel to someone.

All Star
Minneapolis, MN – August 2008

"He sure is tall!" My grandma exclaimed
as if he wasn't there. We we're sneaking out of
my room, trying to exit the apartment without
being noticed – a difficult task when one of you
is seven-feet tall. We'd met on prom when he
sold me lines of coke in the bathroom. He was an
all-star athlete with a coke problem – the first I'd
ever met. He'd just graduated and had been given
a full ride on a basketball scholarship. I still had
two years of high-school left. He never talked
much – I'm not sure he had much to say. Perhaps
he was just shy. Or perhaps he felt awkward
around a grungy gay kid. Regardless, he spent
that summer coming to my house selling me
coke.

A few days after my grandma noticed the
giant leaving my bedroom, he was on television.
He had just robbed a bank in Wisconsin with
another friend of mine. I could have told my
grandma that it was someone else, but his height
sort of gave it away that night on the news when
it flashed surveillance footage of him alongside
his mugshot.

That was the first time I realized the
intersectionality of addiction. He was smart, he
had money, he had talent, he had an entire future
that was fully funded, he had friends, he had
family, and he had his demons. I'd spent my life
being told that addiction was a symptom of

poverty – that I suffered from this symptom, but that night in my living room, I saw first-hand that they were just as fucked up as me. In this case, more so; I'd never robbed a bank.

Infected

Portland, OR – December 2015

I'd been awake for two days when I finally fell asleep watching a movie. I woke up two hours later and my vision was blurry. I could barely get off the couch. I stood up finally and stumbled into the bathroom, where I collapsed on the floor. My nostrils were dry and hurt. My mouth was dry. My eyes burned. I didn't feel like I could breathe properly. I was drenched in sweat. I laid on the bathroom floor and let the cool tile press into my hot, aching body. After gaining enough energy, I crawled on my hands and knees to the closet where I grabbed for a thermometer.

I put the thermometer in my mouth. I began to gag and pulled it out, but not quickly enough. I puked bile all over my body. I took my underwear off and threw them down the hall. I tried again. I sat, waiting, still covered in my vomit. It finally beeped and I took it out, but I was unable to read the numbers. My vision was too blurry. Suddenly the numbers disappeared. I'd taken too long reading them. I tried to take my temperature for a third time. This time I had my phone ready. When it beeped, I took a photo of it with my phone. I zoomed in on the picture so I could read the numbers: 104.6.

I crawled to the tub and began filling it with cold water. I got in and waited for it to fill. I stayed in the cold water, now mixed with my puke, for fifteen minutes. I took my temperature again, my vision was a little better, 104.7.

I puked in the bathtub after taking my temperature. I got out and put on sweatpants and a t-shirt. It must have taken me another fifteen minutes to do this. I couldn't think straight. My vision was coming and going. My hands were going numb. My entire head was tingling. I started crying. I couldn't tell if it was a panic attack or something else. Because of how quickly it came on, and the numbness I was experiencing, I was worried it was meningitis. I tried to call 911 but couldn't read the numbers on my phone.

"Siri, call 911." I said to my phone.

"Calling 911." Siri responded.

"Hello what's your emergency?"

"I HAVE A FEVER OF ALMOST 105, MY BODY IS GOING NUMB, I CAN'T STOP PUKING, MY VISION IS BLURRY, I'M DYING, AND I CAN'T READ NUMBERS."

"What's your address?"

"I'm going to die."

"Sir what's your address?"

"I live at 1800 Park Avenue. I'll wait outside."

"Are you okay to make it downstairs?"

"I think so."

"Okay I'm gonna have you stay on the phone with me. An ambulance should be there soon."

I made it downstairs. I told her I was on the corner of Park Avenue and hung up. I didn't want to die talking on the phone. The ambulance finally arrived. I can't remember the first few minutes, but I remember the driver saying "this isn't an emergency. Ambulances are for emergencies. Have you been taking drugs?"

"Are you fucking kidding me? Take my fucking temperature. This is an emergency."

"No I'm not fucking kidding you."

"You have to take me to the fucking hospital!"

"No I don't."

"This is fucking bullshit. You're gonna get fired."

I walked into the middle of the road, away from the ambulance driver. I tried waving down cars, no one would stop. I wasn't wearing any shoes and it was December. Finally, a car pulled over, just as the ambulance began pulling away.

"Are you okay man?" A guy asked.

"No, I'm not. I promise I'm not crazy, on drugs, or anything. I live in this building and I need to go to the hospital."

"Get in." He said.

I lived only about ten minutes from the closest hospital. He didn't say another word to me, he just drove. When we got to the emergency room, he said "good luck, do you need anything else?"

"No thank you!" I blurted out before swinging open the car door and puking everywhere. I shut the door, and walked barefoot through my vomit into the emergency room.

I went in and gave the woman at the desk my insurance and ID and stuck out my wrist for a band. I knew the routine. She asked me what was wrong, I said "I don't know but I have a really high fever."

She told me a nurse would call me back to get my vitals soon. I grabbed a garbage can and began puking in the lobby – no one paid attention to me. The emergency room is the one public place you can vomit uncontrollably and no one will look at you weird, or look at you at all.

The nurse came out and helped me stand up and handed the garbage can off to someone else. One nurse checked my vitals while the other asked me questions. My entire face went numb and I started yelling "my face is numb, oh my god I'm dying! I can't feel my face!"

"Are you on drugs?" The nurse who was asking me questions said with an annoyed tone.

"Go fuck yourself. No. I'm dying. Check my piss."

The nurse continued writing notes. The nurse who took my temperature passed the thermometer off to another nurse and said "we gotta get him a room, now."

My fever was over 105, and was nearing 106. I continued to hold a bag that I gagged bile into as I was wheeled into a room and put into a bed.

I was hooked to an IV and given fluids. I'm not sure how long I was there, it's all a blur. I know there was concern over my fever not breaking. When I stopped vomiting, I was given ibuprofen first, and then acetaminophen, and then more ibuprofen. This went on for hours. They packed me in ice and eventually my fever broke. They took quite a bit of blood for testing. Then everyone left my room and I laid in the dark while the IV continued giving me fluids. After a couple more hours, the doctor came in and told me they were discharging me.

"What's wrong with me?"

"It's probably the flu."

"Probably?"

He gave me the typical instructions for the flu, and sent me on my way. He said he would call if the results turned anything up. He said the initial results were fine, but to come back in if my fever got high again.

"Tell that nurse who thought I was on drugs to go and fuck herself." I said as I walked into the morning light.

I filed a complaint with Emergency Medical Services that day over the ambulance driver, and requested a copy of my 911 call. I emailed my primary doctor and told him I was dying and had meningitis. Then I slept.

* * *

I woke up to stabbing pains in my stomach. I had shit myself. It was evening. I'd slept for twelve hours. It was 7pm. I made my way to the bathroom, and sat on the toilet for hours with diarrhea, while I puked on my legs. I was crying from the pain in my stomach. I'd never felt a pain like it before. When the vomit slowed down, I lit cigarette after cigarette, and sat on the toilet until 11pm. Every time I tried to stand up, more would come out.

When it finally stopped, I rinsed off and took a Lyft to the hospital, soiling my underwear on the way. I tipped the Lyft driver $50 for the smell.

It was the same nursing staff. I told the lady at the front desk not to let the demonic nurse anywhere near me, and pointed to which one I was referring. She asked why I had returned. I told her my fever had come back, and said "I can't stop shitting."

I was checked in and given a bed again almost immediately because of my fever. I didn't have a doctor, I had a nurse practitioner this time. She was kind and sat on the edge of my bed when talking to me. I told her I was scared and wanted my mom. She promised me I wouldn't be discharged until she had done a full workup.

I eased in this time, and wasn't as panicked. I trusted the woman helping me. She was warm and kind.

I shit myself again and tried to make it to the bathroom. When I stood up, I projectile vomited across the room. I was hooked up to the IV and was too disoriented to figure out how to unhook the drip bag. I ripped the IV out of my arm and watched blood squirt across the room. I started yelling and a nurse came in and yelled "oh for Pete's sake!"

I remember laughing. The room was covered in shit, blood and vomit and her reaction was "for Pete's sake." My reaction would've been more colorful.

* * *

After being given a cocktail of meds, I finally felt better. There had been a mass shooting in San Bernardino and the nurse and I watched the clips of evacuees on the news.

"This world can be so cruel." She said.

I didn't say anything, although I agreed.

The nurse practitioner came back in. I'd been there most of the night. She said "look, you're really young. I'm a mom. I know how terrified I'd be if I couldn't be with one of my kids when they were in the hospital with no idea of what's wrong. I know you're scared. But you're doing better, so we have to discharge you for now, but I have ordered every test possible. So we will have answers for you, and I will personally call you with the results later."

I believed her.

* * *

"Hello. This is the nurse practitioner you saw. I'm calling with the results of your tests. Is now a good time?"

"Yes." I said. I had been studying for a final. That week it was finals week, and I had to pack up and clean my apartment, let movers in, have my stuff driven to Minnesota, and fly back while vomiting everywhere.

"Your stool sample shows that you have a Shigella infection."

"I have what?"

"It's a bacterial infection of the stomach similar to E. coli. It's likely you got it from something you ate, or through oral-anal intercourse."

"Will I be okay?"

"Well usually it clears on its own, but your infection is far more severe and I'm not sure why. We are gonna start you on some antibiotics. You need to make sure you stay hydrated. Also, your results have to be reported to the Oregon Health Department and they will contact you soon to ask some questions about how you might have contracted it."

We talked for a bit longer. A friend drove me to pick up the antibiotics. A few other friends helped me pack. The movers were coming the next day. My professors were lenient and let me submit my finals online. I ended up throwing most of my things away, I was too tired to pack it all.

Like many people in their early twenties, I hadn't made a plan for what to do after I graduated. I knew I wanted to continue with my education, but I was unsure of in what capacity. I had originally planned on driving a truck by myself across the country to store my things in my mom's basement in Minneapolis, but was too

sick to do that. So I hired a truck to do it for me
and bought a plane ticket for the next day.

My apartment was trashed and covered in
the filth of an intense drug addiction. I was scared
I wouldn't get my deposit back. I wrote a note
and taped it on the floor of the apartment that said
"I understand the place is a mess. Sorry about it.
Things happened. I really need my deposit back. I
understand you're probably laughing at the
request right now, but remember that time a girl
was murdered in my apartment before I moved in
and you didn't tell me? [A girl had been
murdered in my apartment decades earlier] And
remember that time when the pipe in the
bathroom gave me a second degree burn on my
ass after I requested three times that it be fixed
and I didn't sue? So I'm really gonna need that
deposit back."

After taping the note to the floor, I went
down the road and I spray painted an exes front
door, before taking a cab at 4am to my friend's
house. My flight left at 10am.

I woke up at noon that day having missed
my flight. I booked another flight for the next
morning and booked a hotel room that night by
the airport. The room was rundown and smelled
of stale cigarettes from the 90's. The vomit
colored carpet made my head spin. I lunged onto
the bed, and stared at the once vivacious paint on
the walls. It was the end of an era. I knew
returning to my family meant the end of my
relapse. It meant the end of my coasting through
life. It meant I would have to get my act together.

My stomach cramped at the thought – or maybe it was just the diarrhea from the infection I still had. I wasn't a kid anymore. I couldn't just show up in the world half present and hope for the best. I had to try.

I passed out for sixteen hours that night. When I woke up, I'd discovered that I'd once again slept through my flight. My adulthood was off to a great start. The signs were saying "turn back while you still can."

The World of the Deranged
Portland, OR – September 2012

Every leaf fell off every tree in one day. That's when it started raining. It started raining and it never stopped. The streets filled with water and I was up to my neck trying to remember how to swim, but I couldn't. I couldn't remember anything. My arms grew tired and I thought to myself, "where the fuck is a life jacket?"

Crazy starts with a flicker; the flicker will soon turn into a flame, turning everything into ash. In the isolation of my darkness, I first noticed my life's ashes building at the tips of my cigarettes. The real world, my world, my sanity and insanity… they all become the same. No one around me saw it happening until I was too far gone for salvage. The day I realized I was crazy, everyone I'd ever known had died. I was the last person on earth, adrift in the middle of the Atlantic Ocean. I was finally alone in the ocean and able to fully submerge myself in this world of delusion; a place where water comes with a side of Lithium, ink blots are not just paint splatters, anger is seen as mania, and silence could put you on suicide watch. Everything you thought to be true is now false – obliterated by your perceived lack of mental competence.

I was walking from my apartment to class when it started. I didn't feel like I was a part of my body. My head was very tight, and I felt above myself. I sat in class and tried to focus on what the professor was saying but I couldn't understand her or piece her words together. I tried to take notes but my hand didn't feel like my hand. I was sure if you cut it off I wouldn't feel anything. I sat in my chair, pinching every reachable part of my body as hard as I could. I pulled strands of hair individually from my head. I bit the insides of my cheeks, my tongue, and my bottom lip. I could feel the pain but it felt indirect. This wasn't my body.

I decided I was just tired. After class I took a nap. I awoke in horror that night to discover I felt the same way. I was convinced I was dying, but didn't do anything about it. I stayed in bed for days.

I woke up one morning a few days later and my throat was swollen shut. I'd never been so excited. I knew what this was. I've gotten strep throat 2-3 times a year, every year, since I was little. I looked at my throat in the mirror and could see the pus on my tonsils. I nearly ran in excitement to urgent care. I was right. I had strep. They gave me the antibiotics and I went home. I was positive the way I'd been feeling was my body trying to fight off the infection before it took hold of me. I stayed in bed and took my antibiotics. Days went by and my throat got better, but the feeling of being out of my body was still there.

Weeks went on and I tried everything: exercise, only drinking water, eating healthy, cutting down on smoking, doing good deeds for others, praying, meditating, all of it. Nothing relieved me of the horrible feeling of detachment. That is until one evening when I was positive I would die, I caved and had sex with a neighbor who had been pestering me for a month or two. During sex, I felt normal. I could think. My head was clear. I was my old self again. I didn't want it to stop despite not being attracted to the person I was with. I was cured... until orgasm. Within seconds of ejaculating the feeling was back again.

The sex alleviating my symptoms indicated that maybe it was mental health related. I'd had some anxiety as a teenager, but who doesn't? Aside from that, I'd never had any mental health issues... that I knew of.

Welcome to the world of the deranged. You'll either die here or be released, but once you've come here, you don't leave – not completely at least.

His Life Mattered
Portland, OR - December 2012

All of the girls loved him. All of the boys loved him too. He was friends with everyone and nice to anyone. He never cared that I was gay. Before the other guys in my high-school accepted me, he was a friend.

I was walking into the cafeteria, carrying my lunch tray. I jolted forward and fell - a surprise hit in the back. A guy in my biology class had shoved me and pretended he hadn't meant to.

"Hey man, not cool. Back off." Collin was sitting at the table I'd been pushed by. He was talking to the asshole who pushed me

"Here man, sit down." He pulled out a chair and motioned for me to sit.

We talked for a while. We had a lot of mutual friends. We both liked coke. He had a good sense of humor. I invited him to come to one of my parties sometime.

My best friend at the time had warned me that he was shady and to stay away. I wanted to see for myself.

* * *

The first time he came over we didn't do drugs or get drunk. He brought some friends and they were preoccupied with girls. He just sat and chilled with me and talked. I remember he was

wearing dress shoes, nice jeans, a baby blue
sweater, with a button up shirt underneath so the
collar stuck out the top of his sweater. I
remember thinking he was dressed nicely for
someone with such a bad reputation.

* * *

I remember the rumors about his drug
use, but I can only remember doing them with
him a handful of times, and we hung out a fair
amount. I think what was said was different than
the reality – it usually is. I didn't see him much
after high school but our paths would cross
occasionally. He was always the same guy. He
had been an accomplice in a bank robbery, but
we never talked about it and I did see him
occasionally after that. He was black and the
other person involved in the robbery was white.
Despite him being a minor at the time and the
other guy being an adult, law enforcement came
down harder on him. As we got older the
differences the world placed on him as a result of
his skin color became more apparent. After the
bank incident, what was he or any young person
of color to do? A good job was unlikely, as was
college.

* * *

The newspapers said he jolted forward
and fell – a surprise hit in the back. A police
officer had shot and killed him as he ran away

from the scene of a grocery store robbery. It was before the black lives matter movement began challenging police brutality while getting mainstream media to notice. His death went unchallenged. The media largely ignored it. Friends said he only robbed the store because he was trying to help others with the money. His death was different than my other friends who had died. I wasn't sad or confused. I was angry, but the anger largely resulted from my disappointment in the world for being so heavy on him. Everything he did was because of some obstacle preventing him from doing anything else. I'd gotten out, but I could understand the things that would drive a person to rob a store. I could understand the mental health, the economic anguish, the addiction – all of the disease and disorder, but I couldn't understand shooting someone who had their back to you.

For me his death represented a numbness many millennials have engrained in them – many doomed from the beginning, forced to accept their demise years before it happens. Why hadn't I accepted mine?

Prescription Prostitutes
Portland, OR – Fall/Winter 2013

I never sold my body for drugs – this reality still surprises me. The thought crossed my mind but I found other ways to support my habit. It wasn't until I entered the world of delusion that I was forced into the sex industry. I wasn't "escorting" in the traditional sense; there were no late night walks on 82nd Ave. There were no craigslist posts advertising "erotic massages" with my photo attached. My experience in trading sex for cash happened very organically.

I've been ridiculed and judged for my statement, "I was forced into the sex industry." My peers have argued that there's always another option. But these peers weren't in need of unaffordable medical treatments. My peers had the ability to have a job, collect unemployment, state health insurance, and disability – resources that for one reason or another, I had been denied. I was on psychiatric meds that kept me from being suicidal. I was unable to afford them. My prescription was almost up, and I knew if I didn't get the money for it, it would end in my death. I was desperate.

* * *

I wanted my bulge to entice them. I watched for eyes darting towards my spread legs in my well-worn Levi's. I was sitting alone in a back corner at a local gay bar, trying to look unamused and a little sad – what I thought would be easy bait for the silver foxes in the room.

* * *

It was almost bar close when his glossy black shoes appeared beneath my line of vision – hands clasped to my face as I looked downward. I looked up and didn't say anything. I left it up to him. He offered me a drink and I declined with a smile – letting him know that he could stick around.

* * *

Leaving the bar, I was sure I'd vomit. It was a six block walk to his hotel and I was sure I'd collapse somewhere along the way. I tried to ignore my thoughts, and focus on what he was saying, when I did, I realized he was just as nervous. He wasn't sexually forward in conversation, and I could tell he wasn't the aggressive type. I had a feeling he was a five-minute-man and vanilla was the only flavor he knew. I could go through with this. Thirty minutes with this man meant a month of physical well-being.

* * *

One John turned into another. I didn't ask or care to know their names. I can barely

remember their faces. From the few men I
"escorted" for, all that's vivid are the looks I'd
receive from the hotel doormen. Men often in
their early twenties, with knowing smirks on their
faces as I escaped the hotel and fled into the early
morning. Over the course of the Summer I would
frequent the high-end hotels of Portland's
Westside – The Nines, The Heathman, The
Benson. I became more comfortable with
escorting, but it became harder to conceal.

It was the first week of September and I
was exiting the Nines, face down to avoid eye
contact with the front desk. I wasn't able to avoid
looking at the doorman though. He'd seen me
two or three times a week for a month – never
had he done more than say hi. Tonight was
different. He turned to the valet,
and smirked noticeably. He'd seen me enough to
know what I was. As I approached the door, he
did not open it. He did not hail me a cab. I
walked home in the rain that night feeling the
lowest I'd ever felt. Would he have smirked had
he known I was doing it to stay alive? I was
surviving. All I wanted was a doctor to fix me.

* * *

After recovering from the incident at the
hotel, I went to the local male strip club and
observed the men working. The combined scent
of vodka and sweat hit me and I was already
regretting my decision to scope out the scene. My
friend was working that evening – he was on

stage and watched me as I sat alone at my table, getting settled. When he was done on stage, he made his rounds flirting with the men who had thrown $1's at him. He sat across from me and scoffed at my visible nerves, "you fuck people for money but you can't handle being in a strip club?" He told me to mingle and flirt.

I stayed away from the younger guys and the attractive ones. They were just there for fun. I was on the lookout for the older unattractive man, alone and sad, drinking his bourbon. There was a group of bearish looking men at a table with an open seat – I observed them a good while before I approached the group. I didn't ask for the open chair, I just took it and was warmly greeted by all but one. The formal introductions were cut short as two of the men started flirting. I went along with it, biting my lip, running fingers through my hair, forcing myself to blush – these two were hooked. The man who hadn't greeted me was still silent and began burning holes in me with his eyes.

He finally broke his silence, "What exactly are you doing here? You're at the strip club alone. You're not dancing. You're not paying dancers. You're not drinking. Instead you're flirting with us, hinting around about what our plans are for the night. Trying to flip a quick trick? What're your rates? I got a $20. Are ya just strung out trying to get a fix of that Tina?"

The man was a complete stranger – never before nor after have I seen him, but his words stuck with me. It's as if he branded the word, "worthless" across my forehead. I ran out of the club without saying goodbye to my friend. I was hyperventilating. I lit a cigarette, and when the coast was clear I cried. *I have no choice.*

Welcome to Hollywood
Hollywood, CA – Summer 2007

I never cared much for the bad reputation Los Angeles gets. The things most people loathe about the city of angels are the things I love it about it. It's the most depressing city in the world. When you go into the restaurants along Sunset Blvd for lunch, the waitresses who work the day shift are in their 50's. They moved to LA in the 80's from Cincinnati and Kalamazoo. Many starred in a horror film, maybe two, before their career ran dry. They wait tables to pay the bills raising their kids. Their dark roots show under their bottled-dyed blonde hair. It's the city of broken dreams and stranded dreamers.

I had run away from home. My father thought I was in Minneapolis with my mother, and she thought I was in Portland with him. I had been staying with friends recently signed to Atlantic Records in the Hollywood Hills. They were a grungy, alternative rock band known for exposing their pubic hair to the audience and falling over drunk on stage.

My first night there I went out with the band. We sat around a dimly lit table, soaking in the wafting aroma of alcohol and sweat. The heavy bass pulsated through me. I attempted to stand and fumbled. Tequila caused my face to stick to the floor. I started laughing, my friends started laughing, everyone laughed – the life of the party. I plunged back to my feet resulting in cheers from my peers. With confidence I continued my stride to the bar, cockeyed with a grin that reeked of whisky. I hadn't noticed my sagging pants that exposed too much.

"Sir! I think it's time the tab be closed," I slurred to the female working the bar.

She stared at me as if deciding whether I would be worth the assault charge or not.

I lifted a knee atop the barstool and leaned over the counter, waiting for the receipt. The room was now dancing in circles around me. The pulsating music was no longer loosening my muscles, but was causing the ones in my stomach to tighten. I knew it was coming. The last whisky sour bubbled in my stomach, rising towards my throat.

* * *

La Cienega Boulevard was the street sign I saw when I lifted my head off the nicotine stained, taupe leather seats. I was in the back of my friends' old brown Volvo, parked a block off of Sunset Blvd. I remember laughing at a man for his outfit, but nothing after that. *Did I puke?* I continued to bake in the heat of the early afternoon sun, watching as waves of it hovered above the concrete. The car grew stuffy, filling my nose with the scent that leather gives off only on Summer afternoons. A chubby, fluorescently dressed Hispanic woman pushed a cart past, advertising fresh tamales. I could have puked. I felt around my pockets and the back seat for my phone and wallet – they were gone to the night.

What the hell happened last night?

I pushed the car door open, extending my shoeless feet into the air before placing them onto the concrete. It was like I was crawling above the ground after being buried alive. I stood waiting to gain balance as my eyes adjusted to the California sun. I felt a sense of comfort as I breathed in the familiar aroma of urine and exhaust, a scent unique to Los Angeles. I slammed the door shut, and made my way towards Sunset. It would be at least a two and a half mile trek up Laurel Canyon before I reached the house with the blue door on Utica Drive – the Hollywood Hills home I'd always dreamed of.

* * *

My time there wouldn't last long. The band was dropped from the label soon. I couch surfed for a bit after that until a trans woman took me in.

A Limbo of Madness
Minneapolis, MN – October 2012

They sedated me.

In my sedation I was told that my lunacy was something that could be controlled. I was told that I was alright when really I was mostly dead. My symptoms were suppressed, but when you're deranged and sedated, you're not living, you just haven't died yet. My mind was in overdrive trying to formulate thoughts – yearning to let this monster out, but forced to keep it in. Those of us who remain crazy and stay sedated become stuck in a limbo of our own madness. I could participate in society without being a threat to myself but I could no longer participate in my life. I just existed in the lives of others, watching helplessly as every part of me slowly deteriorated, eventually becoming nothing.

After I decided to take a year off school to get better, I was given Valium. Then I was given Klonopin, then Xanax, Ativan, and Serax. The goal was to get my panic attacks to stop so that I could leave the house to attend therapy, get a job, and continue going to my doctor appointments so that maybe I could find a drug that wasn't a benzodiazepine to help me out.

Paxil made me stay awake for days. Zoloft made me cry for days, but one day while on it, a snap occurred and I felt normal again. This only lasted for a few weeks before Zoloft quit working entirely. They continued to up my dose and I ended up in the hospital with a suspected case of serotonin syndrome – a rare side effect that can be lethal. If my panic hadn't been bad before, the near death experience increased it to catatonic proportions.

A Peaceful Dance
Los Angeles, CA – Summer 2007

We trudged our way up Laurel Canyon BLVD to a house we had access to – some Hollywood High asshole – also desperate for real friends – who was the product of an 80's teen idol and his Valium addicted wife. No one was home but we snatched the key from under the porcelain-angel-baby they kept by the door. We went to the basement and settled in at the bar. She attempted to mix some drinks – distracting herself from her intense craving while I prepped her poke. I looked up, and through the most lifeless eyes, she looked in desperation at my hands while I utilized a spoon, syringe, and a small piece of cotton.

"You stingy fucking prick! Put a little more in," the once beautiful girl now weathered, screaming, and slapping the bar before turning her back to me. I didn't care that she'd lost it on me, but when she slapped the bar, she'd left a large hand print on it, formed out of sweat from her palm. This girl was sick – sicker than me.

"Fine, but we're splitting this fifty-fifty." I was annoyed with her for prolonging my fix. Gripping her arm tightly with one hand, I began thumping my fingers on it trying to get a vein to surface. After a few agonizing minutes I felt one plump up and pulse against her worn, bruised skin.

"Ready?" I asked, looking into those sad

green eyes.

"Oh yeah." Her eyes still empty.

Pressing the worn tip deep into her flesh, a collision began as spurts of blood erupted into the syringe. I gazed momentarily as the beautiful maroon stream integrated with the junk, peacefully dancing in swirls. I started pumping it into the life lines from where it'd just come. Surging into her body she flung her head back in relief. She was stoned, now it was my turn. I performed the same process, but much faster. I jammed the needle into my arm with the force one uses to put a nail through drywall

* * *

We sat silently for the rest of the night, and a week later she had left Los Angeles without telling anyone she was leaving, or where she was going. I didn't know much about her – our friendship was a bond formed outside of reality, created in the realm drugs allow one to enter. We had never asked each other about our pasts. I didn't have to ask, her eyes said it all – glossed over and cold, as lifeless as a dead body. The memory I have of those eyes, and the way they'd send chills down my back, is an image I will have forever engrained, like the track marks down my arms.

Good Winter
Troutdale, OR - September 2011

The musician Justin Vernon was binge watching the 90's show Northern Exposure when he learned of the French phrase "bon hiver" meaning "good winter." He would name his band Bon Iver and produce melancholy music perfect for listening to while the snow falls.

* * *

I'd been living back in Portland for a couple of months when I heard Bon Iver was coming to town.

* * *

I spent years listening to Bon Iver's album "For Emma," watching the snow fall on Sunday mornings while I came down in Minneapolis - driving through blizzards in silence (except for the music) with friends.

It was a remedy like no other when your dry nose, sore throat, and depleted dopamine made you want to put your head through a window.

* * *

I met a girl in Portland that year from Wisconsin. My roommate had let her into our apartment and when I came home she was laying on my bed. She was covered in tattoos with eyes innocent like a golden retriever. She declared that we we're going to be friends. When I mentioned Bon Iver was coming, she said "I'll drive."

* * *

The morning I took my ACT's in high school, I'd done too much coke.... and Adderall. My lips were turning purple while I took the test and I couldn't stop shaking. I powered through the exam and ran out of the room. When I got to the restroom I realized I had blood streaming out of my nose. I wiped my face off and went to the parking lot of my school. I had my friend's car keys. I got in the car and listened to Bon Iver's "Blood Bank" until the Xanax kicked in and I dozed off.

* * *

Tickets were sold out. We couldn't find any scalpers. The concert was at an outdoor venue. It started raining while we approached strangers in the parking lot, looking for tickets. We eventually gave up on tickets and we danced in the rain while listening to the music roar through the chain link fence. I'd been sober for a year and a half and in that moment it all came flooding back. The cravings I'd had and the aches. My mouth watered for it and my stomach cramped from the nausea of thinking about how much I didn't want it. I felt alive in that moment but wanted more - I was always wanting more. My friends thought I was sitting in silence, listening to the band prepare for their encore. But I was catatonic from the blizzard in my soul. My horrid memories were tied to this beautiful music.

Trees lined the venue. I climbed to the top of one in the rain and watched the last two songs from high above - unfortunately, no branch could get me as high as I wanted to be. The new friend I'd made was great. I was trying to use her to make memories that could hopefully erase the nightmares I'd lived. I was sober but she had no better understanding of me than the friends I had come down next to. Just like back then, I was physically present, but that was it.

That night I began looking for excuses. A little Adderall could help my studies a lot. It wasn't getting high if I was using it to study. I went to bed that night listening to Bon Iver. I left the window open, pretending it was snowing.

Neve Campbell
Portland, OR – 2002/2016

Someone once told me that when there's a full moon, we do in fact act differently, and some people lose it. The gravitational pull from the moon that creates waves also has a stronger pull on the water in our bodies when it's a full moon. That pull puts all of us a little on edge. I don't know if it's true but I like the way it sounded.

* * *

I called her Neve because she looked like Neve Campbell. We had our first kiss behind the school gymnasium on the first day of summer. She was my first girlfriend.

We had our first fight later that day - she slapped me as hard as she could. I cried a little. The slap had occurred for no reason. She was the sweetest girl on earth most of the time but would turn on you in a second - catching you in her storm of rage. No basement was deep enough to hide from these tornadoes.

* * *

She wasn't in class one day. Sarah wasn't in class. Emily wasn't in class. A few other girls were also not in class. Mr. Elm was in a weird mood and instead of teaching he put on Bill Nye the Science Guy.

At lunch the rumors began to trickle in. The girls had been with the guidance counselor all day. Johnny Loren said he heard they'd been caught fingering each other in the bathroom. Dennis Kessler said that was a lie. He said they'd been smoking cigarettes in the bathroom.

When we heard the truth, it had nothing to do with a bathroom. Neve's older brother - who also looked a little like Neve Campbell - molested her. Not just her, but half the girls in our class. Not at the same time, or even in the same night but over the course of two years. Whenever Neve would have a friend sleepover, he would target her. When she didn't have girls' sleepover, he went for Neve. Neve never slept over at anyone else's house. Her parents were too strict. No one was allowed to sleep over at her house anymore after that day - the day Sarah had told her parents what had happened and half the girls were pulled from class.

Neve and I grew apart and we never really talked about what happened. I later admitted to being gay and she joined the track team. Neither of us could accept the others new extracurricular activities.

Neve's brother didn't go to jail. I heard my mom gossiping over the phone to Steven's mom one night. She was pissed. His family and their church had decided to pray the pedophile out of him. None of the girls ended up pressing charges.

A year after high-school, I was watching the news with my best friend Riley. She and I had stayed friends since kindergarten. Neve was on. A few blocks away in Milwaukie, Oregon, she'd stabbed a girl twice in the chest. There had been no altercation and no motive. The girl collapsed with the knife still in her – illuminated by the full moon in the night sky. I wasn't shocked – I just shrugged. I could understand why she was so angry. She fell through the cracks; everything and everyone had failed her.

Unlovable
Portland, OR – Spring 2014

I was late to our first date. He was waiting for me in the sun that rarely appeared in Portland in the Spring, sitting on the waterfront of the Willamette river. We spent the afternoon walking around, before he came back to my place to help me put together a couch I'd bought. He wore a baseball cap, a bleach stained t-shirt, and cargo pants. He looked like a boy scout with Mick Jagger lips. We kissed on the floor after finishing the couch. When our lips separated, he let out a gasp. I knew he was in love with me.

* * *

On our second date, we made dinner together. I decided to make salsa, and accidentally got jalapeno in my eye. The burning was instant and quickly spread to the rest of my face. We spent the remainder of the date with him pouring milk in my eye, and rubbing a stick of butter on my forehead. When I got out of the shower after the burning had finally stopped, he was still there. He'd gone to buy more milk, "just in case" I needed it.

My friends loved him, he was kind, he was gentle. If I gave him a book recommendation, he would stay up all night reading it so we could talk about it in the morning. He ate wherever I wanted to eat. He watched whatever I wanted to watch. He cried when he was sad, and went on walks when he was angry. He always asked me "how are you?" and "can I do anything for you?" When I started using coke again, he choked back tears as he said "it's gonna ruin you. I just want you to be okay." He would miss work for me; he walked through fire for me.

I would stay up all night, spun out on amphetamines, chain-smoking, and he would just hold me. It terrified him.

He thought I was brilliant. He always wanted to read what I was writing. I could murder someone and he wouldn't let go. Nothing I did was ever enough to scare him off – which was all I wanted to do.

When I looked in the mirror I saw a monster, fueled by depression, panic, and cocaine. When he looked at me, he saw someone who was lost and just needed to be loved. The more damage I did, and the meaner I was to him, the more he loved me. I would make fun of him, I would flake out on him, I would sleep with as many people as possible, I would consume so many drugs it was impossible to have a coherent conversation with me. He loved me madly. He never did drugs, and he never drank around me. He made sure I would sleep, and he made sure I was eating.

This went on for months.

He would write poems on empty cigarette packs, napkins, and scraps of paper left around. I kept all of them.

I decided I was gonna get sober. In my clarity, I realized I'd completely ruined his life. I had a desire for him that I'd never felt. No one had ever taken care of me before like he did, I'd always done it by myself. Most of his friends had left Portland, but here he was stuck. I was all he had in Oregon and I was garbage. I had to learn to take care of myself, and to get my act together. I couldn't do that with him around. He was about to go home for Thanksgiving. He came over to say bye before his trip.

I told him to stay in Michigan. I said he couldn't come back to Oregon. I told him I didn't want him. I said it was over and to stay away from me. I kissed him like I was dying, and gave him a hug that made my body feel it would deflate until I was nothing. When the door to my apartment closed, I collapsed on the hardwood floors and cried for five hours. I had to stand alone now. I had to fight my problems on my own.

* * *

He flew to meet me in San Francisco two years later, but I had relapsed again and refused to see him. I wouldn't even answer the phone. So he flew back to Michigan.

* * *

He flew to meet me in Portland a few months after that, but I was still using. I talked to him on the phone and told him not to follow me and that I didn't have time. So he flew back to Michigan.

* * *

To face him would be to face all of the horrible things I am capable of doing to someone. To face him would be to face my ability to throw love in the blender and watch it turn to mush, and then try to snort the mush.

Baltimore

New Orleans, LA – September 2015

I walked through Congo Square in Louis
Armstrong Park collecting discarded miniature
rainbow flags. Southern Decadence – an annual
pride festival in New Orleans - had just passed. It
was 90 degrees and the air was sweating on me.
A large raindrop broke through the heat and
plopped on the back of my neck. Within seconds
a storm of biblical proportions took hold of the
city. I ran into the entryway of the Municipal
Auditorium, taking cover. I lit a cigarette and
observed the wreckage from Hurricane Katrina.
The auditorium had opened in 1930, and for
decades remained an elegant venue for music.
Now, ten years after Katrina, the building stood
haunted from the beating the hurricane had
delivered.

Two men broke through the rain and their
silhouettes stood in the entryway, they turned
their backs to me and watched the storm. They
both looked homeless. I took photos of the
boarded windows covered in graffiti.

"Hey can I get one of those?" The short,
fidgety one turned to ask me. He wanted a
cigarette. I pulled out my disintegrating pack –
soaked from the rain – and handed him one. He
said thanks. He had his own lighter. After a few
puffs he handed the cigarette to his friend – a
bald man in a tank top and jean shorts that hung

below his knees. I continued to kick through the rummage of stones, boards, and litter.

The bald one kept watching the storm and held onto the cigarette. His friend directed his attention at me.

"Where are you from?"

"Portland." I said "and you?" Although his accent had told me the answer.

"I'm from New Orleans. What're you doing here?" He continued to fidget. His eyes looked like they were coming out of their sockets. He smelled sour, and was sweating profusely. I'd guessed he'd been up at least three days. Meth.

"Just looking around." I lit another cigarette, and sat down on the steps leading to the door of the auditorium.

He turned to his bald friend and said "Man I need to sleep. I'm starting to see shit man, and my chest is killing me."

"Pass out here." The bald guy finally spoke.

I asked how long his chest had been hurting, asked what kind of pain it was, and other general questions about his health. The bald man sat down on the steps beside us. While I talked to his friend, he pulled out a razor and began shaving off his eyebrows.

"Here take this." I took a pill bottle out of my backpack and handed him a Klonopin. He took it without asking what it was.

"What is that?" The bald one asked.

"Klonopin."

"Can I get one too?" I handed him one.

"Thanks. My name's Baltimore." He stuck out his hand.

"I'm Dalton." His friend said.

We sat talking about New Orleans for a half hour before the rain cleared. His friend curled up on the steps, using his backpack as a pillow. When the storm cleared, Baltimore and I walked back into the park. We left Dalton sleeping on the steps.

"Nice meeting you man, take it easy." He said before we walked our separate ways.

* * *

It was around 1am. I was sitting at a park off of Decatur Street overlooking the Mississippi River. Four men approached me from behind.

"Got a dollar?" I didn't see which one asked.

"No. Sorry." I kept looking at the river.

The guys stood behind me, talking amongst themselves. I felt uncomfortable. The entire walkway was empty but they stood directly behind me.

"Where you from?" One of them asked.

"Portland." I didn't break eye contact with the river. I had a bad feeling.

"What's in the bag?" One of the men reached over the bench and picked up my backpack.

"Can you not grab my bag?" I stood up and faced them finally – not seeing another option. I could see two more figures walking up behind them.

"Can you not grab my bag?" One of them mocked me.

"Hey, he's cool, leave him alone." One of the shadowy figures walking up said. It was Baltimore. He was with a friend, not Dalton.

The guy dropped my backpack on the ground. Baltimore and the four other men talked for a minute. They knew each other. I lit a cigarette and went back to watching the river – trying to be casual. The four men eventually walked away, leaving me with Baltimore and his friend. I'd never been so relieved in my life.

"You're pretty stupid you know that? You shouldn't walk around this part of nalins by yourself at night." Baltimore said while lighting a cigarette.

"Hey baby, I'm Tucker." His friend stuck out his hand. He was a lanky southern boy, probably around 19, and had purple rimmed sunglasses on at night.

I was taken back by him calling me baby, but he had a warm presence, despite having the swagger of a used car salesman. The three of us walked alongside the river together before venturing back into the heart of the city. We walked from destination to destination while Baltimore sold meth out of a fanny pack around his waist. We did this for a couple of hours before Baltimore asked to use my phone. We sat on the steps outside of someone's house while he used it. I took out my polaroid camera and took a photo of him. I'd gotten in the habit of taking photos of everyone I met. He looked up.

"Is that okay?" I asked.

"Sure." He broke a smile and then went back to my phone.

Tucker and I continued talking. I found out he called everyone baby "so I never have to remember anyone's name" he told me. Eventually Baltimore stood up, but stayed fixated on my phone. I didn't mind. He'd saved me after all. Tucker lead the way and we continued through the city. At some point my phone died and Baltimore handed it back to me. The sun was about to come up. We stood on a side street just outside of the French Quarter while the two of them smoked meth. I watched. I was tired and needed to board a plane in a few hours to head back to Portland.

* * *

The backs of the seats on the plane had a USB port to charge your phone. Mine was still dead from Baltimore using it all night. I put my bag under the seat in front of me and plugged my phone in. It started up before the plane was fully boarded. Out of curiosity, I wanted to see what Baltimore had been doing on my phone all night. I had a few minutes before I had to put the phone in airplane mode. I went onto the internet and looked at the history...

Man Wanted for the Murder of Police Officer.

Woman Sexually Assaulted in French Quarter.

Tourists Murdered in Atlanta.

There were also searches for a name – next to the name was his mugshot.

The intercom interrupted my pounding heart "please turn off all large electronics, and make sure phones are turned off or on airplane mode."

Waterlilies
Minneapolis, MN – March 2010

I awoke in yet another backseat of
another car - a habit I'd formed over the years.
It's evening and I can't stop shaking. I lie here,
watching snow fall before a neon sign
advertising "Full Service Gas Station." It's the
first big snow to hit Minneapolis this Winter.
Lifting my head, I'm hypnotized by the powder-
covered-parking lot. *It looks like cocaine.* A
parking lot filled with pounds of cocaine; my jaw
can't help but clench at the thought.

Through the window I see my buddy
and the clerk we'd inevitably befriended through
countless hours of killing time in that parking lot
– waiting for drugs, a party, or a place to crash.
This is the first time I've ever enjoyed the snow.
It's probably the heroin. I'd just smoked prior to
nodding off. I'd inhaled the tar, watched a cloud
form as I exhaled, and nodded off to the comfort
of it flowing through my bloodstream. I still feel
the warmth – the love it gives. My brain's
become a prison, maybe *Sing Sing*, all of the
inmates – my endorphins – are escaping. It's their
first breath of freedom after years of
confinement.

I can't stop shaking; I've been shaking
for five years. *Maybe it's hypothermia?* I'm
lying in a car, hidden beneath blankets of
white. *What will my skin turning blue feel
like? Will I suffer amnesia or get naked? I've*

heard people remove their clothes during hypothermia. Will I remove mine? Maybe I should just take them off now, to ensure that everyone knows I've suffered both in life and death. I'll become a cautionary tale of a wasted youth.

This is it. Do I or don't I? I could die tonight and it wouldn't be suicide, it'd be my loss of ability to keep fighting. I could live tonight. I could do this again tomorrow, but maybe tomorrow will be the day I'm brave enough, strong enough, and willing enough to finally fight and beat this. To never stop loving drugs but to learn to live without their love in return. I can feel my body slowly closing the blinds on my life. I have to make this choice, now.

I took what I thought would be my last breath, and slung open the car door, extending my bare feet into the harsh winter air before placing them firmly in the snow. I didn't say anything to my friend – there was nothing to say. I needed shoes, my toes had passed pain and numbness: I no longer felt they existed. I tried to move faster but my body was more rusted than the Tin Man. I walked home.

I was alone standing before a print of a painting I had that I'd stared at on acid a hundred times, but this time, I understood it. In my most vulnerable state, I willingly sacrificed myself to the artwork. I was absorbed by Monet's *Waterlilies*. I lost direction and was lost amongst the lily pads but no longer fearful – the clarity of the water beneath those lilies began to cleanse me. I floated amongst the blossoms, wondering if I could drown in this painted lake. Could I get up, walk into the painting, allow the deep blue to fill my lungs, and drift into unconsciousness?

I was baptized by Monet, in the water beneath the lilies. I didn't need Jesus, God or any religion for this sacrament. This was a sacrament to myself – my allowance to be admitted to a life that could be enjoyed. I was willing to sacrifice to be able to live again.

Peeling off my clothes I observed the grayish figure that stood before the bathroom mirror. The stomach was sucked in enough to allow every protruding rib to be counted from a distance. The once white teeth were now dark-yellow. Dark bags circled the emotionless, bloodshot eyes. Nothing was there anymore.

I cried through the stomach cramps on the floor. I moved to the tub when the vomit started spewing through my nose and out of my mouth, covering my entire body. The bile that rose from my gut left an acidic odor that caused my stomach to tighten and release with every breath. I began to regurgitate more chunks of the unknown onto my cold, shivering skeleton. I lay there, shaking uncontrollably, trying to turn the handles on the tub. That's when the bugs came. Each centipede began to furiously make their way through my body, moving beneath the skin's crumbling surface – feeling every bite as they ripped through my flesh. I frantically tried to scratch, tear, and pull them out. They had the upper hand, forcing me to claim defeat. My tear ducts hurt, my stomach hurt, my head hurt. I'd never felt a pain like this but at least I was feeling. I gave up on the bugs; I let them crawl to the surface and make small holes, before going back under.

When you're stoned a month feels like a minute, but when it's leaving your system a minute can last several years, maybe even the rest of your life.

Nice to Meet You
Portland, OR – October 2015

I was on my way to the pharmacy to pick up my prescription for Lamictal when I realized my biggest fear yet: the loss of self. I've always been wild, spontaneous, fun and creative. Who was I without my highs and lows? They say I am Cyclothymic - I don't exist without it. After picking up my prescription, I sat on my bathroom floor for hours just staring at the bottle. If I took this pill, my entire life could be digested with it - the bad and the good. If I didn't take the pill though, eventually, and soon I thought, my life would be lost to insanity. I'd started smelling gasoline randomly throughout the day, along with other weird delusions.

It was the hardest decision I've ever had to make. It was time for me to bet my entire identity on a chance at life, at happiness. I would have no idea who I was without my swings, but I would be dead if I kept them. I was no longer willing to play Russian Roulette with my life. I clutched the sink with my clammy palm, staring at myself in the mirror one last time. I placed the pill on my tongue - still using the sink for support. I took a final deep breath, and swallowed. It was then that I looked at myself again, nodded in reassurance and said,

"Nice to meet you."

The Itchy Asscrack of Miami
Miami, FL – October 2010

I'm hopped up on Viagra and Nicotine, wanting nothing more than to wipe away the puddle of sweat dripping from the small of my back to my now itchy asscrack.

"Cut! Stay where you are! John I can see the fucking mic on camera, move it! Okay from where we left off."

Sweat wiped, ass still itchy.
Fuck.

Where we left off was me hunched over the back of a couch, knees firmly planted in the cushion with my ass out, and my right hand tightly grasping my now sore manhood.

Remember what he said, keep your head down for a moment longer with your eyes shut before finally flipping your hair back, letting out a soft moan.

I continue to stroke my dick – pretending I'm alone in my bedroom. With my back arched still, I lifted my head, flipping my hair back.

"Uhhhhh," I let out their moan.

"What the fuck was that? Who's gonna get off to that? That was the least believable moan I've ever heard!"

College
Boca Raton, FL - Fall 2010

Freshman Year: Day 1

Free from high-school, I wanted to go somewhere new. I pointed to a spot on a map, and Boca Raton was where I landed. I was a freshman in college in South Florida, post-release of "I'm in Miami Bitch." I hadn't realized what I'd gotten myself into until I arrived on campus and was greeted by a Haitian chauffeur in a golf cart. His name was Charles – he acted surprised that I shook his hand and introduced myself. No one else had. Charles would become a friend during my time there. He helped me take my bags to my dorm and gave me a quick tour of my new home.

It was a country club guised as academia. A playground with tight security for the rich and reckless. I was among the elite: heirs, politician's children and royalty even. It was the 1%. The parking lot reflected beams of light from the hoods of foreign cars. I was sure the swimming pool was a casting call for the next Sports Illustrated Swimsuit Edition. My first night there I went to an ABC (anything but clothes) party where a bottle intended for one girl made its way around the party. Thirty or so people were consequently roofied. I was the only one concerned over the incident.

Freshman Year: Day 80

"Get up! What're you two doing? It's Wednesday! And I've got a plan!" Riley burst through the door with Jenny, drunk on Four Loko (two months before it was recalled for killing people). She was in baggy sweats and a white undershirt she'd no doubt stolen from a guy's floor as she snuck out of his room that morning.

"It betta be a plan for this fuckin' animal. I told ya Riley that Eight Ball aint livin' with me. I don't giva shit if he was Julian's pet. He shoulda gotten a normal fuckin' pet like a d'wog." She had gone from Jenny to Jersey Shore – her New Jersey accent always more thick when angry. Eight ball was a gerbil a friend had pawned off on us, and we didn't know what to do with it.

"It is! Bogie is passed out with his window open!"

I leapt up, now riled at the thought of seeing Bogie pissed in the morning after waking up to a gerbil. I could see it now: Him making his way to our smoking spot, moving faster than his usual sloth pace, yelling at us in that thick South Boston accent. His calm demeanor had infatuated us, and we lived to see the rare comedic moments he got worked up.

"I like this plan. Those two belong to each other. They both got stupid fuckin' names." Jenny said as she grabbed the gerbil from it's cage and handed it to Riley.

"Take the fuckin hamsta. We're not carryin' a fuckin' cage around campus. This aint a goddamn Petco."

"It's a gerbil, not a hamster." Riley and I laughed.

Freshman Year: Day 2

Anton - my wealthy roommate from Prague - and I made it to the furniture store on nothing but my bad directions and his broken English. It was our second day in the Florida sun. The store was packed with other freshman scrambling for dormitory necessities.

An employee approached us.

"Hey you guys here from FAU also? We have a delivery service for first year students."

FAU was another university within proximity. The question left Anton's face scrunched in confusion.

We said we went to Lynn.

"Ohhhhh haha you guys are Lynn kids."

Lynn kids? This time it was my face that scrunched. *What does that mean?*

I later found out these remarks were normal from West Palm Beach to Fort Lauderdale. The school had made headlines that year for losing students and faculty abroad in Haiti when a 7.0 magnitude earthquake hit. These headlines prevented us from seeing the notoriety that normally surrounded the school. Pretty soon the antics of the wealthy and wild would once again steal the spotlight from the catastrophe, but when it would, it was too late for us to not get swept up in them.

Freshman Year: Day 80

We crept into the darkness, fearing the moonlight would reflect from our albino friend – the gerbil - and give us away. We made our way towards the edge of the swamp on campus and pretended to pay attention to the geese.

"What're you guys doing? You goin out tonight?"

We'd been spotted. Our mission had been compromised. It was Alexander.

"Just thinking of swimming! Ya know?" Riley twisted her body towards him, placing one hand on her hip, while slipping the gerbil into her sweatpants with the other. Her trademark crooked, drunk grin spread across her freckled face.

"In the swamp?"

"Oh sure. You know. The geese here are nice cause everyone feeds them." Somehow she kept a straight face. That was Riley. I doubted it was the first time she'd had a gerbil in her pants. Had we not been on a mission, swimming in a swamp wasn't something I'd put past her. Alexander had invited us out with him. We were on a mission, so I quickly changed the topic.

"What's the deal with that?" I pointed towards where we'd just come from. Ricky and Celeste were holding hands entering the dorms. *A drunk mistake?* I wondered.

"Oh you don't know? Alexander explained "Celeste said Donny was a slob, and left him. But she really left him for my boy

Ricky. Who's also sloppy." Alexander always knew what his "boys" were up to. It never seemed to include him - I think that was his choice though.

"Well let me know if you guys wanna come out." He turned from us and jotted toward where Ricky and Celeste had gone. Riley let out a sigh and pulled the gerbil from her waistband.

"My pants are not your new home. These aren't even my pants. You aren't even my gerbil." She said to our furry friend.

"Come on Dr. Doolittle. We got shit to do." Jenny said.

We made our way across campus, greeting drunk friends in passing. I continued to be preoccupied at the thought of Alexander. I felt bad we didn't take him with us. He would've called us immature though. He was good looking, nice, smart, and a member of Manhattan's elite. I'd hated him for those things initially, but I realized he was different. I got the impression he was living a life of obligation. I'd met a lot of kids at Lynn like this. They were mini adults. Years later I would see him in the New York Times with a full page spread. He was the youngest CEO in the world of luxury watches. He inherited the company from his father. He had been prepped his entire life for the job.

We were almost to our destination, but our glowing white friend was a bug zapper and the intoxicated were flies. Out of the darkness they swarmed us, wanting to play with the gerbil, but as we made it closer to our destination, the flies dwindled - as if fleeing something sinister in the dark.

He was coming right for us, we should've followed the flies. His greasy hair was matted down. He wore a shirt he'd been wearing and sweating through for a week - his pants hung close to his knees.

"Hey fuckers! What're you assholes doin? I took a bunch of fuckin' K and Molly cause fuck tonight." DJ Donny Don't Stop had stumbled right for us. He was loud and rude. He was always claiming to be high on Ketamine and Molly. I wondered how much was true and how much was an act for attention.

"Did you guys know about Ricky and Celeste? Am I the only one who didn't?" His slur was gone. His ability to go from messed up to normal was one reason I suspected it was all an act. Before we could answer he continued - he always did.

"I mean I don't care if you guys did. I'm not mad. It's cool. Screw that slut, and fuck Ricky."

Donny had insisted everyone call him "DJ Donny Don't Stop." He said it was his stage name. Apparently he was a really famous DJ up North. A famous DJ that never performed, or made music the entire time I knew him.

"I just heard that. That's so fucked up. I'm so sorry." Riley's guilt in having led him on earlier that semester prevented her from turning away with Jenny and I. We sat on the ground and waited for Donny's rant to be over. When it continued on, and an end seemed unlikely, Jenny and I got up and walked away from Donny and Riley unnoticed. We could see the light on in Bogie's room. The window was still open.

We could see him - fully clothed - spread across his bed.

"Think he's knocked out?" I popped my head up and took another peek into the room.

"Hey Bogie, you dumbshit, you asleep?!"

"Nice Jen. Get security called on us."

"You check then."

I began to whisper "Bogie, psst Bogie" through the window, when Riley barricaded past us, Eight Ball in hand, and went torso first through the open window. An ungraceful fall was met by a bed of empty beer cans. The noise was enough to wake up anyone. He didn't flinch. He was passed out. Riley gave his back a shove. Nothing. Jenny had a loud New Jersey howl for a laugh - when it mixed with my cackle, we were a siren in a tunnel. We covered our mouths as we watched Riley rub the gerbil on Bogie's head. No longer able to hold in our laughs, we turned and ran - leaving Riley to massage Bogie's face with the gerbil.

Freshman Year: Day 76

I'd added another life to my list of growing identities. I had the friends that partied - who I went out with. I'd also made a small group of friends that were easier to be sober around. They were studious, and like me - were only able to attend Lynn University because of scholarships. Going through the local papers one week in search of stories regarding my peers, I was surprised to see a giant photo of myself in the Broward Palm Beach New Times. It hadn't been the negative commentary that most of my peers received. The headline read "Quidditch Tournament at Lynn University," and the photo was of me and a few friends - suited up and holding broomsticks. We'd recently honored Harry Potter and took our fandom to the field to play the sport from the film. Living so many lives and trying to keep each separate saw an end on November 15th, 2010. This was one side of me that I was proud to have the world see. It was the only side I liked. It was a side I'd just began developing. A photo in a local paper might not be exciting for most but it was for me. It was my reward. It was the first time I was acknowledged for doing something innocent.

Freshman Year: Day 80

Riley didn't come back that night. She'd find us in the morning with a new story of her wild night. Jenny and I stayed outside chain-smoking, and guessing where she'd ended up.

Ricky and Celeste emerged from the door they'd disappear through earlier. They crept towards us how we'd crept across campus that night. Crouched down, looking right to left, exaggerated mannerisms. For us it had been a comedic impersonation of a spy; for them it was an attempt at being nonchalant in their drunken stupors. We laughed thinking they were making fun of us. But then Ricky loudly whispered

"Yo you guys seen that psycho Donny?" His Brooklyn accent was thicker than usual and his brown Puerto Rican skin was pale and sweating.

"Not for a while. What's wrong?" The urgency in my voice matched his, out of concern but mostly excitement over the thought of them being caught in bed by Donny.

"He wants to fucking kill us. He's been looking for us all night. He's been texting Celeste fucked up stuff. We've been camped out in my room."

"He was so fucked up when I saw him, he's probably blacked out by now. You guys should be fine. Besides you know how dramatic the famous DJ Donny Don't Stop is. The guy is full of shit." I'd gone from concerned and excited to annoyed at the lack of drama.

"Okay well if you see him tell him we left campus for the night"

"Will do man." My words must have calmed him because he didn't imitate the Pink Panther walking away from us like he had approaching us.

"Where the hell do you think Riley ended up? She doesn't have her car keys does she? That girl needs to be more careful. She does so much dumb shit when she's drunk." Jenny barely finished her words when - as if this were a play - Donny appeared from around the corner. His glistening forehead and dilated pupils let us know that he was no longer exaggerating how high he was.

"You guys seen that slut and piece of shit?" He paced towards us like he was gonna take a swing.

"I don't know slut and piece of shit." Jenny matched his attitude.

"Ricky and my sloppy seconds, Celeste." Donny calmed his voice, he knew if anyone would punch him, it'd be Jenny. He stopped inches from us, staggering before hunching to catch his balance. He wouldn't look at us and his eyes darted around – paranoid of something nonexistent. I tried to picture what the world looked like to him right now - but I'd only done Ketamine once and it was nowhere near the amount he'd obviously done.

"I'm gonna kill those assholes. Blow their fucking brains out. Fuck everyone at this school. They all can get shot. Everyone knew about them. Everyone. Everyone they. They... fuck Ricky. And fuck Candice."

"You mean Celeste?" Jenny had to taunt him.

"That's what I fucking said. You guys are cool. Don't worry. But fuck all these other assholes. They all deserve it. If you see them, come find me." After a few tries Donny finally stumbled in the right direction towards the door.

"Didn't he just meet Celeste last weekend? What a fucking baby. He always wants sympathy. Just lookin' for another goddamn handout." The real Jersey Shore was out - not the amplified version she does when she's screwing around. This was the one that had a no bullshit policy, even if it wasn't directed at her.

November 2012

Don't get me wrong - I'm glad I eventually left Lynn. It wasn't a bad place. I had some great professors and friends there. Not to mention the beautiful campus. It just wasn't for me. However, I sometimes miss the excitement. The people who surround you there... Their presence alone makes you feel important. At least it did for me - for a while. I remember staring at the TV in envy years later as I watched Obama debate Romney there. The friends that still went there were all in attendance. They, or their parents I should say, were considered *important* enough to get them seats and arrange the debate on campus. I kept thinking "I could be watching this in person right now."

Freshman Year: Day 81

I passed out on Jenny's floor that night. When we woke up we went outside to watch the walks of shame and smoke our morning cigarette. We hadn't taken Ricky's fear seriously the night before. We hadn't taken Donny's behavior seriously. When we opened the doors to go outside, it was obvious that we should've taken the threats more seriously.

An RA approached us through the crowd of gossiping students, police officers and journalists. She started talking to us as if we should be shaken by the scene. We were only 18 and we were already jaded by the frequency of mass shootings in America. The RA walked away from us, and before we could finish saying "what the fuck" another approached. The school staff made their rounds, students gossiped, police questioned, and journalists snooped. I can't remember how Jenny decided to handle it - but I feared the judgment of having been naive enough to not take a threat with a gun seriously.

I'd told people I'd been off campus that night, and a journalist - who later would pester me on Facebook - that I'd never met Donny. He knew I was lying. I wanted to distance myself from my naivety the night before. Thankfully no one ended up getting shot. We listened to the rumors before seeing the bold letters filling the front page of the paper "Donny Sanders Threatens to Inflict 'Columbine Take 2' On Lynn University Students." Like any good millennial, Donny had taken to social media to live update the world on his plans to open fire on our campus. How'd we miss his status updates? We logged on to read his three posts from the night:

"It's gonna be Columbine take 2"
"just purchased the ruger SR9c 9mm"
"just registered for my firearms license hahahahahaha get scared..."

He didn't get as many likes as I'm sure he was hoping for.

Amidst the circus outside, we spotted Riley across campus - wincing at the sight of sun, and the cluster of frenzied people. From across where Riley was standing emerged Bogie. He ignored the discomfort of light after a hard night - he was on a mission.

We could hear him yelling from where we were sitting. "Yo! What the fuck!" He made his way across the lawn to Riley. "I woke up with Julian's fuckin' rat c'walin round my bed and shit. I was about to bust into your room. It's screwed to put a rat in a bed with a pa'son. I could have got rabies and died." His angry South Boston accent ignited Jen's howl, prompting my cackle. They could hear our laughs from where they were standing - two buildings down - and slowly turned to meet our eyes through the chaos. The western style duel was it for Riley, the queen of keeping cool. Bending over in laughter, she finally broke character.

Freshman Year: Day 103

I was leaving for the Miami airport and grabbed the local paper as I walked across campus one last time. I would leave Florida for good. I exited campus, leaned up against the security gate that had remained closed since the incident with Donny, and unfolded the paper, waiting for my cab.

The headline read "Lynn U Soccer Player Dies in fall from Bridge." That was it. One final reminder of the world I'd been living in since moving to Florida. I had earned the reputation of being a Lynn Student - enough to make a store employee say "oh you're Lynn kids."

As for eight ball, Bogie had let him into the hallway that morning. Sightings of him were reported by residents throughout my remaining time as a student there.

Thighs of Heroin
Phoenix, AZ – Summer 2006

"Is there anything besides the pot?" The officer had me backed against the car. His forehead had three deep furrows imprinted from a lifetime of serious expressions and Arizona sun. He was scanning my face looking for a hint of something. I didn't answer.

"I said, is there anything besides the pot?"

There's three ounces of heroin taped to my thighs.

I could feel the sun high above Tucson turning the back of my neck pink.

"Look, you seem like a good kid, and don't have a record. These guys aren't worth ruining that for," he continued, speaking as if I were his child. "So if there's anything you're not telling me, now is the time to say it."

The fat one said somewhere around Scottsdale that I have a big mouth and has since been jokingly pointing his gun at me. But if I say anything, it won't be a joke.

"No," I responded, looking him straight in the eyes. I was hoping he would give the driver a ticket for possessing the bowl with res in it and we could be on our way. I pictured myself rotting away with twenty-five to life in some jail cell in Tucson. I would have a cellmate. He would sweat a lot; he would have no teeth; he would smell.

It was in this moment that I might have

set the record for worst time possible to break into laughter, but when I saw the police officer's dark-blue, fake alligator-skin boots, all I could think of was that line in Romy & Michele's High School Reunion when in reference to Tucson Romy Says, "we're like the only ones who don't look like we're going to a hoedown."

I bit the inside of my lip hard enough to instantly taste blood. I stopped laughing. The officer leered at me, tilting his head as if looking over the brim of some non-existent pair of aviators.

"Sorry, I laugh when I get nervous. I just am hot and tired, and a little scared of cops."

The officer sighed and lifted his head, ending the *Walker Texas Ranger* impression, he said "Look, I'm going to have to take the driver in, but the three of you can continue on. I don't want any more trouble while you're in Arizona. Ya hear?"

I could have shit.

That evening we would finish our drive and arrive back in Los Angeles. I sat in the backseat, while the fat one continued to joke and point his 9mm at me. He knew I hated guns and loved to taunt me with it. More stops were planned but the cop was enough to scare everyone into holding their piss. My stomach cramped the whole way home, and I would break into cold sweats randomly. I only found relief once we hit heavy traffic in LA's urban sprawl. I'd never been so happy to be dead-stopped on a highway.

An American Teenager
Minnetonka, MN – Fall 2009

- 5:45am:

- Alarm
-30mg Adderall XR with a sip of Red Bull
-Go back to bed

- 6:15am:

-Adderall wakes me
-Cigarette #1; Line #1

- 6:30am:

-Shower

- 6:50am:

-Glass of $8 Vodka
-Line #2
-Go on my morning walk. Cigarette #2

- 7:00am:

-Chain-smoke on street corner waiting for my ride to school.

- 7:45am:

-Arrive at school

- 12:30pm:

-Leave at lunch w/ friend.
-Park at gas station.
-Line #3.
-Chain-smoke.
-$8 Vodka – Glass #2
-Take 30mg Adderall IR

- 2:35pm:

-Leave School

- 3:00pm:

-$8 Vodka – Glass #3
-Snort a Percocet
-Line #4
- 10:00pm:
-I'm home. Coming down. Staring in the mirror.
- 11:00pm:
-I start my homework.
-2mg Xanax

Canned Food
Minnetonka, MN – December 2006

She wrote her name – Joanie – on
everything. She was a cashier at the grocery store
I was working at. I was a bagboy. She wrote her
name on her can of soda, she wrote it on the
marker she kept at her register, she wrote it on a
pack of rubber bands next to the marker at her
register, she wrote it on the People magazine she
left in the break room, she wrote it on her purse,
on her wallet – literally, everything.

Aside from writing her name on
everything, she seemed normal. She was a
stickler for the rules, and told the manager on you
for everything. One time I didn't tie my shoe
right away, and she told on me and said it was a
safety hazard. She was overbearing and didn't
have friends. Her life was rather sad, but you
don't always think about things like that when
you're fifteen. I definitely didn't.

I had befriended another bagboy, Chad.
We went to the same school and were in the same
grade. He gave me drugs for free, and we took
them on break together – 2cb, ecstasy, acid,
shrooms. Whatever we could get. He liked to
pick on Joanie. One day when the store was
getting ready to close up, we ran around it with a
marker and wrote "Joanie" on easily 100 food
products on the shelves. We thought it would be
hilarious. There she would be, scanning groceries
the next day, and suddenly all of these products

would appear with her name on them. Maybe she would get how annoying it was that she wrote her name on everything.

Chad was bagging for her the next day, and I was in the lane next to him. I saw it before he did… a can of soup a customer had gotten had the name "Joanie" written on it. I couldn't contain myself. I started chewing on my lip to prevent myself from laughing. My laughter was getting harder to control as I watched the can of soup slowly move closer to Joanie on the conveyer belt. I tried to pay attention to the customer I was currently bagging for. I didn't really care about them at this point. I was watching brilliance unfold.

Joanie grabbed the can and went to scan it. I looked at Chad, he looked back, I nodded toward Joanie and motioned scribbling with my hand. He understood what I was saying. He saw the can. Joanie was just staring at it and staring at her name written on it. He burst out laughing – caring much less than I did about concealing our identities. He ran to the bathroom, laughing too hard, his face was dark red. Joanie was still staring at the can. I began to feel uneasy. There was a pit in my stomach, and it was riddled with anxiety. I felt bad. Maybe this would hurt her feelings. *Do I tell her it was me and apologize?* She finally put the can in the bag and continued scanning.

* * *

Chad quit working there and Joanie quit writing her name on everything. After the holidays Joanie stopped showing up for work. I asked our coworker Katrina what happened to her. She'd taken a leave of absence. She had slit her wrists on Christmas with the lid of a can of cranberry sauce. I'm not sure if that was true or not, but it's what Katrina said. Katrina might have known we had written "Joanie" on numerous cans of food in the store, and said it to make us feel bad for screwing with her. But she never indicated that she knew about it, or knew Chad and I had done it. As far as I knew, she really did try to kill herself with a can.

* * *

I had quit working there shortly after. Chad and I had stayed friends. We saw each other at school. During photography class, we would sneak out and go and smoke pot in the parking lot. We only hung out outside of school sporadically. When we did, we did mountains of cocaine and ecstasy. He sold coke for a bit, and would sell me eight-balls for cheap.

* * *

I began to see him more when he started dating a friend of mine, a girl I rode to school with. It was odd to me that they were dating. Before they started dating, she had never done drugs, never had sex, got straight A's, and was quiet and reserved. All of that changed, and quickly. Chad was sent to rehab and transferred out of our school. I shared homerooms with his weird stepbrother and would occasionally ask about him. His girlfriend was devastated. They never even got to say goodbye. She would sit alone, quietly in the cafeteria. As the school year went on, I watched her slowly disintegrate. She said she was fine, but she wasn't.

* * *

Chad returned from rehab, and eventually came back to our school. He and my friend started dating again immediately. They were doing more drugs than ever. There were copious amounts of coke and we were doing it before, during, and after school. I heard he was doing heroin, but I never saw it myself.

* * *

No one had heard from Chad for a few days. His girlfriend and two of our friends went to his apartment to try and figure out what was wrong with him and why he wasn't answering his phone. They found him on the couch with a bullet hole in his head. The gun was still in his hand and there was a note.

I left school to go and console his girlfriend. As my friend and I ran up to her at Lake Calhoun to hug her, she let out a shriek like nothing I've ever heard. That sound left a scar on my eardrums and I'll hear it forever. I watched as she collapsed and cried.

* * *

Sitting at his funeral, I wondered if he thought about Joanie while he was contemplating suicide, or if he'd forgotten about her. I went into the grocery store a few years ago when I was in town and saw Joanie working the cash register. I ended up turning around and leaving. I think she saw me, but I'll never be sure. I also thought I could see a scar on one of her wrists.

The Dark End of the Tunnel
Minneapolis, MN – December 2012

White.
I blink.
White.
I continue to stare.
A ceiling.   My vision is coming to.
I pop my ears.
Am I under water?
Muffled voices graze my eardrums but are unable
to penetrate.
I'm under water.
My ears must be water-logged.
The tickle is growing stronger. I know it's
going to hurt but don't know why. The air pumps
out of my lungs. My cough sends my chest
lunging forward.
Gasping. My stale cigarette breath – now
accompanied by whatever I'd hacked up from the
depths of my lungs.
I inhale harder. The air is forced through
mucus and enters my lungs. I can taste the snot.
The bitter scent of vomit has entered my nose.
The pain sends me lunging from the bed.
Sharp. Tight. My whole head feels like someone
is driving shards of glass into it.
I've come to my senses.
My arm is squirting blood like a
Tarantino film. I think I ripped out my IV.
There was an IV in me? Why the fuck was
there an IV in me? And where am I?

Trying to find someone is too taxing – I know if I try and get out of this bed, the pain's gonna make me collapse.

I don't stand a chance.

* * *

I almost died and when I did, there had been no light at the end of my tunnel – no pearly gates, no out of body experience, no flashes of my past. It was just dark and seemed to go on forever. I remember feeling scared while I was unconscious, but I was without any actual thoughts – just dreadful emotions. For a few weeks I convinced myself that I had actually died and was in hell – it wasn't hell though, just the life I'd tried to leave behind.

I had survived my attempt at suicide.

The Death of Reality
Minneapolis, MN – November 2012

The burning started and the ash was forming. My handwriting had become childlike, harder to read by the day. I would cry hysterically because the stoplight turned red or the store was out of strawberries. I'd stay awake, sometimes for four days at a time. These small fluctuations – personality defects, became common, and more alarming… anything could set me off. I set a guy's curtains on fire, an attempt to make him feel the burning I felt when he slept with someone else, and to show the burning I'd felt before that, and to show how he threw gasoline on an already unmanageable flame. I ended up putting the fire out – I wasn't homicidal. We broke up that day. I left half my heart and his half-burned curtains in his house that day.

Others were starting to notice my changes, but my mental health was fine. They were wrong. There was something wrong with me physically.

I would soon suffer from my first stroke. Not long after, I would experience a pounding ache in my chest; my first heart-attack. A few months after recovering from my heart-attack I would go into a full blown seizure in the parking lot of my work.

There was this tingling sensation that started in my fingertips and worked its way up. It wouldn't be long before the entire left side of my body was overcome by numbness, affecting everything from the side of my face to my leg.

The heart attack would take place next while I sat in the last row of bleachers watching a high-school soccer team. A dull ache would form in my chest, leaving me breathless. The familiar numbness would shoot down my arm, sending me into a state of catatonic disbelief: It was happening, I was dying. These were the warning signs that I'd heard my entire life. That night I would receive my first EKG.

The last nearly fatal attack on my body would take place two months after the heart attack. My hands began to tremble slightly. I would feel a warm rushing sensation pump through my body that began to burn the surface of my skin. The warm sensation would cause me to almost lose control of my bladder and bowels. I lost control, spewing vomit, and then dry-heaving for twenty minutes. This would be my first seizure.

In all three cases I would be told that the symptoms were entirely real, but that the condition was not. The CT showed no signs of a stroke. The EKG showed no signs of a heart-attack, and the seizure would be dismissed as a figment of my imagination

"You're having panic attacks" they all said.

The doctor's telling me this didn't prevent me from visiting the emergency room sixteen times in the next nine months. I began searching the area for new emergency rooms. If I went to the same one multiple times, they would stop running tests and would give me a referral to psychiatry and discharge me. Or they would make me wait eleven hours, ask me if I was on drugs, and then tell me to leave.

After using all of the emergency rooms in the state of Minnesota, I started driving to Wisconsin. A doctor there told me "I'm not giving you any benzodiazepines if that's what you're after." I opened my backpack and pulled out four bottles of different benzos before saying "does it look like I need any of your fucking meds? I need answers and I need to get better."

My discharge sheet that day said I was suffering from fatigue.

One day when I didn't have my pharmacy in my backpack, I started to have a panic attack. I went to the urgent care to try and get a prescription for two Ativan. The doctor said no. I grabbed a stapler off the nurse's desk and asked "if I staple my eyelids shut will you give me a fucking Ativan?"

They called security and my name was flagged in their system. I began using fake names at the emergency room.

With Every Great Ribcage Comes Great Responsibility
Minneapolis, MN – December 2012

I want my femur to snap in half when I stand. I lay in bed scratching my now bloody kneecaps - pissed they don't stick out as far as my hips. The fat won't leave my fucking knee. I roll over, sick of looking at my stomach. I eroticize the thought of my shins splinting with every concrete-planted-footstep. My desire to be frail has become a sexual fantasy of myself. I want my eyes to bulge out as my mouth sinks in. I want to hear my fucking hips rattle as I climb stairs: an animalistic warning that I'll sink in my fangs.

I'm fucking sick. I'm fucking sick and I know it and I don't care. I want to be weightless - something everyone else views as gross is something I have to have. No fat, no flesh, no skin - just bone.

I doubt my choice in sobriety - coke and Adderall would make this all easier. Without them I am hungry. I am tired. I can't leave bed. With them, I wasted away but didn't have to feel the pain. Weight loss had once been as easy as removing the straw from my mouth and sticking it up my nose.

My little cousin is nine. She weighs eighty-three pounds – I fucking hate her for it.

I want the clavicle of a small child - bare and sticking out.

At some point in my sobriety I developed a strong fascination with thigh gaps and collar bones. I wanted my hip bones to stick out like my protruding ribs – all twenty-four of which could be counted at a distance during the height of my drug abuse. When I quit having cocaine with a side of Adderall for breakfast I was disturbed as I watched the number on the scale grow. I was five-ten and had ballooned up to one-hundred and forty pounds. I had become accustomed to weighing just under one-twenty, and was not happy when my size 26 jeans didn't fit.

It was hard for me to eat during the day - my stomach not used to digestion often disagreed with anything more than an apple or piece of toast. This is where the problem developed. My amphetamine-driven anorexia was paired with insomnia that didn't fade along with my bad `habits. My days spent avoiding food were followed by nights full of tossing and turning. These frequent movements were comforted by binge eating.

My body began to reach what medical doctors would call a healthy weight… I know this now but at the time I considered myself a fat-lard, and was prepared to take drastic measures to get back to my heroin chic self. I didn't feel comfortable expressing this to anyone. There was embarrassment over being male but wanting my body to be tiny. I didn't bring it up in the twelve step program I'd been going to. I didn't know if other men struggled with this sort of thing. I also didn't care – I just wanted my body to stop changing, and wanted to stop gaining weight.

Eventually I couldn't bring myself to look at my reflection. Not just because of my body either. My reflection became my biggest enemy.

Every mirror in existence is in used condition after one person has looked in it. I look in the mirror every day and look at the reflection in it - it's used too. I have lines that came too soon from doing lines off my reflection, and ice pick scars from picking at my skin. My reflection is used because I was used by the speed I was using. I saw a dermatologist once for my scars and he said I had "speed skin." After weeks of hearing the mirrors screaming "speed skin" at me, I smashed them all. Every mirror represents every bad thing I've ever done. Every scar on my face is attached to a memory of the scars I've left on others. Every mirror is used and tells me I'm used. I couldn't handle looking at them anymore. A reflection can be lethal to the insane, deranged, and depressed. And if you're all of those things, and can't handle your body either, well good luck.

Hipster Tweaker
Portland, OR – September 2006/2015

Hipster Tweaker Tied to Actor Evan Anders Death is Jailed was a headline on Vice that morning. I scrolled past. I'd seen Evan Anders in a few movies but didn't care much for celebrity gossip. I checked my email, and then text messages. I signed on to Facebook. I had a few unread messages from people I wasn't connected with on social media.

The first one read "Hello, my name is David Steinberg. I write for Buzzfeed. I saw that you are Facebook friends with Carter Ellison. As I'm sure you're aware, he's recently been connected to the death of Evan Anders and is suspected of selling him the heroin he overdosed on. I was wondering if you had a comment, or any knowledge about Carter Ellison's involvement. I can quote you anonymously."

***

Carter Ellison was one of the first people I met when I changed schools. He'd heard I liked drugs and I'd heard he had them. He was getting some ecstasy for some girls I'd met on the bus, and I asked if I could join them. They texted him.

When we got to school that day, he met us in the hallway and asked if I had $10 on me. I said yes and gave it to him. He said to meet him at his locker during lunch. We didn't know much about each other and he didn't seem to care. I knew the girls he was getting ecstasy for and trusted them, and they had said he was reliable.

During lunch I met him at his locker, he opened it, and pulled out a container of mints. He opened the tin and handed me a pink pill with bunny ears on it – pink playboys.

***

The next message was from a journalist at Huffington Post. "Hello, I saw you liked Carter Ellison's current profile picture. I was wondering if you knew him well. I would appreciate any information you could give me."

I hadn't talked to Carter in years. I wasn't sure why journalists had reached out to me. I didn't even know he was living in Chicago and had no idea he was running around with Oscar winners. He hadn't done heroin when I knew him but it didn't surprise me that he was doing it now. I clicked on his profile and his current photo. It had only been liked by five people – I was one of them. This would explain why I was being messaged. I didn't respond to either message.

***

We never clicked as friends, and eventually I found better and cheaper drugs. We always got along when we saw each other. He never seemed to be at school. He would appear at lunch and sit at our table when it was nice out. He came by to see if we wanted any coke, and sat down and picked at our fries. His eyes were empty, like his personality. It was an emptiness I've now seen dozens of times. I guess that's what happens when you start taking ecstasy at fourteen. I wondered, "am I empty too?" After we'd all decided against buying coke, he left.

***

The third message was from some gossip blog, asking the same questions. I didn't respond. I kept stalking Carter's profile. He never updated his status, and maybe once a year would add a photo. He had just disappeared in high-school. There were rumors he had been shipped off to rehab. It obviously didn't work. He took a plea deal and received probation. He ended up violating his probation and was given a year in prison. I hear he's a comedian now – the emptiest ones usually are.

The Road to Hell
Wanaque, NJ – June 2011

While I was in New York I decided to
visit a friend I'd made down in Florida who lived
in Jersey. Everything I knew about New Jersey
I'd learned from The Jersey Shore. I missed my
friend and was excited to hear her voice as it said
things like "wooder" instead of water. I noticed
as the bus crossed state lines that Jersey was a lot
greener than I expected. It was really beautiful – I
guess that's why they call it the garden state.

When I got off the bus Jenny was
standing next to her car smoking. She ran and put
her arms around me.

"How ya been? I'm so glad you're heuh."

We caught up for a minute outside her
car before getting in.

"So what is there to do in Jersey besides
what I've seen on the Jersey Shore?"

"There's everything to do in Jersey.
Whatdya talkin about? Haven't you ever heard of
Weird Jersey?"

"No. That's Portland's slogan - keep
Portland weird."

"It's a book and I think a website with all
of the weird, crazy, haunted stuff in Jersey. We
have more than most places. Like the Jersey
Devil and Clinton Road."

"What's Clinton Road?"

"It's a haunted road where a lot of weird
stuff happens. It's close by. You're not supposed

to drive down it."

"Have you ever driven down it?"

"Hell no."

"So we're gonna go down it tonight?"

"What is wrong with you? Hell no."

"What's so creepy about it?"

"Well there's this part down the road called dead man's curve. It's a sharp turn out of nowhere with water beneath it where supposedly people have died driving on it. I guess if you throw a penny over that bridge at midnight a dead kid that drowned in the water below throws it back at you."

"Do you have any pennies?"

"Hell no!"

Since I'd gotten sober I'd turned into an adrenaline junkie. I would do anything to make the dopamine in my brain fire. I wanted to be terrified, mortified - I wanted to fear for my life. I'd started doing things like driving recklessly, having compulsive sex with strangers - anything to feel something extreme. Having pennies thrown at me by a dead kid sounded perfect.

* * *

We got to her house. It was beautiful. I'd met most of her family down in Florida when they were visiting, but now I was meeting the rest. They were all loud, opinionated, and hilarious. They had the sort of house you felt welcome in immediately. You didn't hesitate and wonder whether you should take your shoes off or not. The kids called their parents by their names.

We sat by the pool smoking cigarettes - her Newports, me Marlboro 27's. Her family was in the pool, and I kept finding ways to bring up Clinton Road. Jenny side-eyed me every time I did. Each member of her family had a different story - all of which they swore were true and happened to someone they knew or someone they had gone to school with.

In between their stories, I read about the road on my phone. It was ten miles long, no streetlights, not frequented by traffic, and was sporadically patrolled by police. The folklore was grand: the woods surrounding the roads were frequented by witches, devil worshipers, and the Ku Klux Klan.

The road itself was plagued by ghosts, demons, and creatures of the night. Large portions of the road were unpaved until recently.

"Don't fuck around on that road." Her dad warned. "Or if you do, don't get caught by the cops, and come back and tell me everything."

I looked at Jenny. "Fine we can go but don't say I didn't warn you. But I don't wanna go tonight, let's go tomorrow."

We had to go right away. I didn't want her to back out. "What else are we gonna do?" I asked. "You don't have a fake ID. We can't go to bars or a club. Also, I don't want to go to a New Jersey club."

The famous hitman and serial killer Richard Kuklinski, also known as the Iceman had once hid bodies in the woods around Clinton Road. There was a castle that had fallen to ruins a few miles off the road. There were sightings of phantom vehicles, and hellhounds.

"If we get killed by devil worshipers, it's your fault." Jersey said.

"We'll be fine. I always considered myself a little satanic."

* * *

We started off down the dark road with our brights on. There were no people or cars. Dirt became dust and flowed through the high beams - resembling a fog surrounding the car. It was twenty minutes till midnight.

"Where's dead man's curve?" One of Jenny's two friends who came along asked.

"It's a couple of miles up the road I think. We'll know when we get there."

I sat in the back with Jenny. Her friend Brad drove and his girlfriend sat in the passenger seat. My palms were sweaty in anticipation.

We got to the bridge and the girls waited in the car while Brad and I approached the bridge - each clutching a penny between our fingers. I taunted Jenny, heckling her to get out. Much to my surprise she caved.

"Who's got a fucking penny?" She said.

It was 11:56. Four minutes.

When 12:00 flashed across my phone screen I held the penny and motioned throwing it twice before taking a final breath and tossing it over the railing. Bats were in my stomach. My heart was stampeding.

Nothing.

We let out a laugh and sigh of relief. As much as I had wanted to be terrified, the anticipation was enough to curb my risk-taking desires for the night. As I turned I saw Jenny's friend in the car by herself - her face a silhouette from the headlights that were blinding us.

We approached the car and Jenny stopped "did you hear that?"

"Stop fucking around" Brad kept walking but I could tell she'd heard something. Her Jersey Summer tan was now void of color.

I stopped, we stared at each other. That's when I heard it. Someone in the woods close by was playing guitar - gently plucking the strings. Brad stopped but didn't turn to face us. He just said "I heard it." We sat in silence for a moment before I decided to break it by saying "this shit's way too deliverance for me - let's go."

We ran for the car. Brad hopped in the front seat and did a 180 before our doors were even closed. We booked it back the way we came.

About a mile before the main road Brad slowed down. We could see something up ahead - it looked like a fire. We approached with caution, each looking out the window closest to us.

"What the fuck." Brad whispered as we got closer.

Next to the road there was a bonfire but no one sitting near it. In the time we drove to the curve and drove back, someone had come, set rocks in a circle to make a fire pit, filled it with wood, and lit it on fire.

The fear and confusion I was saturated in was a new sort of despair and uncertainty. It was a feeling I would one day be overcome with – the difference is that right now I had a catalyst for the emotion, this wouldn't always be the case.

Hollywood BLVD
Los Angeles, CA – Summer 2015

We ran into Fubar to use their photo booth in-between lines. I still have the strip of photos it printed off. A guy from *The Office* had been sitting at a table. I winked at him and blew him a kiss, he laughed. I had relapsed that week and we bought a quarter ounce of cocaine. It was a small group of us doing it. When we left the bar, we walked back to my friend's place. When we got there, we stood outside smoking. A man in a Hummer pulled up and asked us if we wanted to do any coke. The two girls I was with laughed and said no. I jumped in his car and shut the door. He took off before I noticed he wasn't wearing any pants.

One hand was on the steering wheel and one hand was on his dick.

"You want some coke man?" He asked – completely neglecting the fact that he was masturbating.

"Yes." We were almost out of coke back at my friends and I was desperate for more. We cruised down Hollywood BLVD. Part of me was glad the windows were tinted. The other part of me wished they hadn't been so that maybe someone – ideally a cop – would see what was happening. I would rather be in jail than in this car.

"Okay let's do some man." He pulled off Hollywood BLVD, and we drove into a

Walgreens parking lot. He opened the middle compartment between the seats and pulled out a baggie. He put a book on his lap, set the baggie on it, and started banging away at it. That's when I noticed…

"Dude, that's crack. I'm not crushing up crack and snorting it."

"Do you want to smoke it?"

"No, you said coke. I don't do crack. Have a good night." I went to hop out of the car.

'Sit your ass back down." I closed the door and sat back.

He put the baggie and book away, reclined his seat, flipped over onto his knees and began spanking his ass.

"You like this ass man? Go ahead and touch it."

I had put myself in some situations before, but no other life events came to mind that compared to this. I didn't know what to do. I reached out and poked his butt cheek.

"Nice." I said, as I stared straight ahead – not looking at him.

"C'mon, give it a good swat."

I smacked his ass.

"Harder man."

"I have an idea. Let's go find an ATM, and I'll pull out cash and we can buy some coke. Then I'll smack your ass some more."

"Oh yeah, you're a dirty boy, I bet you like spanking daddy's butt." He wiggled his butt, and then flipped back over and started the car.

We drove down Hollywood BLVD. One of the girls texted me and asked if I was alive. I told her what was going on.

"OMG GET OUT. YOU'RE GONNA DIE." She texted me back.

"Any suggestions?" I replied.

"Jump out of the car on a busy road and run!"

I was tempted, but scared. I put my phone back in my pocket and grabbed the door handle. This is the only time in all of my time in Los Angeles that the car I was in didn't get stuck in traffic or at a stoplight.

"You're gonna be a dirty boy and spank my ass red tonight." He said.

"Oh yeah. Sure am." I played along.

"Let's go park somewhere, we can get coke later." He suggested. We were turning back around on Hollywood BLVD and driving in the direction we'd come from.

"I have a better idea. Let's stop at an ATM and I'll get money and buy us coke and then I'll snort it off your ass."

"WHERE ARE YOU?" My friends texted me.

"Okay man let's do that. He pulled into a 7-11. I didn't wait for him to say another word, I jumped out of the car and yelled "be right back!"

I ran into the 7-11, and without turning around I ran into the area for employees only. The guy at the desk yelled at me "no public restroom!" I kept running. A steel door with an "emergency exit only sign" was in front of me. I barged through it and came onto an alleyway. I ran a street ahead, parallel to Hollywood BLVD, and ran in the direction of my friend's place. When I finally had made it back, they were outside smoking.

"Go inside now! Go!" I yelled as I ran towards them. They ran inside and I followed. I locked the door. I told them everything that happened. Within ten minutes the Hummer was parked outside of their place. We peaked through the blinds and watched him. He stayed out there for hours. We initially were scared and debated what to do, but eventually we forgot about him and went to bed.

Crystal Meth(od)

Portland, OR – November 2014

I started looking for new ways to support my drug habit. It was getting expensive and my savings had depleted.

I met a man who lived close to me with a habit of shooting meth. He was head of a large company that had something to do with tech. I accepted an invite to his apartment one night, and upon entering he was sitting in a jock strap, shooting crystal meth. He'd recently had liposuction and the surgeon had done a poor job tucking the skin after the procedure. So I was captivated by patches of excessive skin that hung down like wet jackets on a coat rack. I couldn't see his nipples as they hid behind the flaps of skin that were recently filled with fat. When he showed me where they'd entered him, I was surprised by how small the incision scars had been - I would expect them to be larger.

On his bed sat two young guys - they looked to be about eighteen. I wondered if they were freshmen from the local university or if he had picked them up off the street with the promise of a fix. They were sharing needles - I cringed.

I didn't participate in their orgy, and I didn't partake in their drug use. Meth wasn't my thing. I was strictly there on business: I had to assess the situation.

For weeks the man hassled me for sex.

He promised me money, drugs, and gifts. I refused but remained flirty; I didn't want him to lose interest.

When my money was really low, I went to the local candy shop and bought clear rock candy. I crushed it into smaller pieces and put it in a vial that was tinted blue.

I texted him "I have an eight ball of crystal; do you want it? I'll cut you a deal."

He said "yes."

I told him I was in a hurry, so I couldn't come up to his apartment. He met me by the fountain downstairs. I had put the vial in a gift box. When he approached me, I said "happy birthday!" and gave him a hug. When we embraced, he slipped the money in my jacket and I gave him the gift box. I told him to have a good night and we parted ways.

When I was out of sight, I ran. While running I blocked his number from contacting me. He'd never had my full name. I just had to make sure he didn't see me around town.

He couldn't call the cops. He also wouldn't find me and do anything to me: he was a prominent man. I only had to worry about him paying someone else to do it and even that didn't really phase me. I now had a new career. I wondered "is this even illegal?" Surely cops would care less than someone actually selling drugs.

I didn't just sell drugs. I promised old men sex, and made them pay me outside "before the act." When they gave me their money, I would run.

The only time I ever actually sold real drugs was in the parking lot of a Taco Bell. A guy was buying 200 Xanax off of me. We met in a Taco Bell parking lot in the middle of the day. He told me to get in his car - dumb move. There were two other guys with him. *I should've had him get in my car.*

"How much is it?"

"$600" I said.

He asked me if I was sure about the price multiple times. I didn't cave. I went to grab the handle and get out of the car.

"Fine, $600 it is." and he gave me the money.

Although everything worked out fine, I realized drug dealing wasn't for me. I was too small and very against firearms of any kind. That was the beginning and end of my actual drug dealing career.

Heartache
Portland, OR – Fall 2015

I'd relapsed on coke and was doing more than ever. I was older now, had more money and resources, and had enough medical knowledge to keep myself alive. I'd stolen a handful of prescription drugs like Propranolol and Lisinopril. When I would take too much Adderall and too much coke, I would take part of a Lisinopril and Propranolol to keep myself from overdosing. Then I'd take an excessive amount of vitamin c and activated charcoal to try and flush some of the amphetamine out. Then I would eat, take a Klonopin, and sleep for a few hours before doing it again. This went on for months. I concealed it from my friends for the most part but eventually people started to make comments like "you're getting too skinny."

I would schedule doctor appointments for no reason. One day I did this for my mood swings - likely caused by speed and sleep deprivation - and when I went in, I did six lines of coke in their bathroom. When the nurse took my blood pressure it was 156/90 and my heart rate was 127. I said I was dying, denied being on drugs, and ended up on Lamictal.

The dose of Lamictal is gradually increased over a few weeks until a therapeutic range is reached. It began to slow my pattern of thinking; I wasn't as impulsive. I was a little easier for my friends to be around. I slowed on the drugs a bit, was sleeping more regularly, and I had started eating again. I was still taking Adderall but eventually I stopped going to class. Then I stopped leaving my apartment altogether. I stocked up on art supplies and religiously painted watercolor self-portraits, took hundreds of photos of ashtrays, and began to make mason jars that represented a different year in my life. I thought I was stumbling onto something genius. Looking back, I really had just taken the same photo of an ashtray three-hundred times. I was no Georgia O'Keefe, but I thought I was.

One evening after I had used all of the memory on my camera taking photos of cigarette butts, I decided I was in the midst of a great project and needed another boost to finish. I picked up some blow, went to the local vitamin shop and picked up L-Tyrosine and Phenylalanine to give the speed an extra kick. I grabbed a few energy drinks and went home.

I added the photos from my camera to my computer and began taking more photos of my collection of cigarette butts. My chest started to ache a little. I assumed it was from how many cigarettes I had smoked. When my left hand went a little numb, I told myself it was a panic attack starting. I didn't want to take an Ativan because I was on a creative roll, but I couldn't let the panic ruin my train of thought, so I caved and took one. I waited but the pain in my chest got worse. I checked my pulse and my blood pressure (with a monitor I'd bought from the drug store). Both were high. I took a Lisinopril. I'd read in The

Merck Manual (a diagnostics book I'd since memorized) that propranolol shouldn't be used in cocaine and amphetamine overdoses as it could lead to breathing problems. I took another Ativan and nothing happened. I took more Lisinopril and nothing happened. I grabbed my stethoscope. I'd been practicing with online audio files for how to listen to heart problems. Something sounded off. It also sounded more faint than usual.

By now it was morning. I searched online for Urgent Care's with an EKG. There was one close by. I took a cab to it, and told the doctor I needed my heart examined. I paid out of pocket and he didn't complain. He ran the test. I'd had dozens of EKG's done and I knew it was taking longer than usual. The doctor came back in.

"You don't need to go to the emergency room but..."

I cleared my throat. The moment between "but" and the rest of the sentence seemed to last an eternity. I thought *fuck I've really done it this time.*

"...your PR interval is off, and I'm going to schedule you a follow up with a cardiologist."

Every other time I'd gone to the hospital or urgent care, my EKG was normal. This time it wasn't. I'd finally damaged my heart. I was 24 and I'd damaged my heart.

Devil Worshipping
Portland, OR – October 2015

"Adderall will work better if you take Tyrosine, L-Dopa, and Phenylalanine. It also helps if you alkalize your system first. I usually just take a bunch of antacids before I take Adderall." I told her while trying to find my money.

"What're those first three things?"

"Supplements that help promote dopamine in the body."

She took my cash and gave me my cigarettes. It was the beginning of my budding friendship with my local convenient store clerk.

* * *

She'd shaved off her eyebrows, so I could never tell what she was thinking. She was also monotone. She told me she worshiped Satan. Her boyfriend had gotten her into it. I asked if she sacrificed animals.

"Not yet."

I couldn't tell if she was kidding.

* * *

I didn't have class and had to get a ton of writing done. I needed to stock up. When I went into the store, she said "hey this is my boyfriend Voldemort."

"Hail Satan." I said, not making eye contact but holding up devil horns with my hand.

"Right on man!" He thought I was serious. I couldn't take someone who called himself Voldemort seriously - you never can.

I grabbed twelve Red Bull, twelve packs of peanut butter cups, and went up to the counter.

"I need a carton of Newport's also."

Her boyfriend cut in "hey man, we tried those supplements you recommended. They worked. What are you? A doctor?"

"No but I've memorized most of the books you need to memorize to become one."

It was true. I had memorized several medical texts one Summer when I was bored and on speed.

"Right on man! She has to work until the morning but do you wanna come to our place and watch a movie I made?"

"Do you have speed?"

"Yeah man of course."

* * *

He took off his pants immediately. It was to get comfortable, he said. His apartment was right out of a Lifetime movie. It was every exaggerated cliché of a devil worshipper you could think of: all of the furniture was red or black leather. There were no actual lightbulbs, but black lights, and a strobe light. On his wall hung a large poster of Aleister Crowley. I asked him "I thought you were a devil worshipper? Crowley was a Satanist."

"I am, but Crowley still rocks." He said.

"That he does."

We snorted some speed. I'm not actually sure if it was speed. It was orange. I'd never in my life snorted something orange, but I didn't hesitate. It wasn't beneath me to snort an unknown substance. We've all had plenty of nights where we accidentally snorted crystal pcp. He turned off the black lights, but left the strobe light on. He pulled out a projector and pulled down a screen for it – I liked his old school aesthetic. I imagined this is what Jimmy Page's house looked like in the 70's. I saw the runtime listed on the play-bar right before he hit play: 4 hours and 17 minutes. I will remember those digits forever.

The first twenty minutes of the black and white film you are just observing hooded figures walking away from the camera. There's no sound. There's no music. Suddenly the film becomes colorized, but in a grainy, high contrast way that looks like it had been filmed with an old super 8 camera. The color footage showed his girlfriend (no eyebrows) sleeping. There was footage of Voldemort shaving. This is when Voldemort pulled out his penis and began masturbating. Nothing turns on a man like watching his own film. I noticed he had a Prince Albert – the definition of cliché.

Voldemort continued to jerk off for the rest of the silent film. One hour of the film had the camera positioned out a window while driving on the highway. I wondered if Voldemort would climax when the film's climax happened – but no, he nor the film had a climax. When it was done he put his pants back on.

"It's like five am. I'm gonna go home and get some writing done." I told him.

"No you're gonna stay." He stared at me and didn't move. Like his girlfriend, he had no expression, despite still having his eyebrows.

"No I'm gonna leave, and you're gonna stay." I turned to walk out of his apartment, with my keys in my fist, expecting him to stop me – the orange powder had me on edge. He didn't though. He let me leave. I avoided the convenient store after that. I could walk an extra block to the next one.

I didn't see them again. I suspect they changed their names back to Jennifer and Doug when the drugs wore off. She probably has eyebrows now and lives in the suburbs.

His Apartment

Minneapolis, MN – April 2011

I shuddered sitting on the cold toilet seat - too tired to stand while peeing. My bladder is full to the point that it's difficult to get a stream going. I hold my breath - it begins. I look out the window - it's a rare sunny day in Portland. *Spring's finally here.* You can hear more people outside than usual. I reach into my pocket for my phone while the stream continues.

"Shit!"

It's 11am. *He's gonna be back any minute.*

I jump up, getting piss on the floor. I pull up my pants and run out of the bathroom. I turn down the never-ending hallway of empty cans, crushed chips, crooked picture frames, and maybe a condom or two.

"Wake up!"

My friend Sandra, still in drag, is passed out sitting upright on the couch. I start gently slapping his face.

"Bitch what?" He groans as he opens his eyes and one of his fake eyelashes falls out of place.

"We have to go. Now."

"Why?"

"The guy who lives here is gonna be back any minute with his wife."

"What?" He jumps up and grabs his heels.

We start to collect his things.

"This dudes got a wife? And I thought you said it was cool we were here."

"Yes, he has a wife..." I say as I pick up a half empty bottle and shove it in my backpack. "...and he doesn't exactly know we are here."

"You said you were housesitting! You have a key!"

"I'll fill you in in a second. Just go."

We run out of the apartment. In the hallway Sandra stops me.

"What about that guy you brought back last night?"

"Fuck. He's still in bed sleeping. Fuck it. Leave him. I don't even know his name."

We run to the elevator and slap the down button frantically.

On every floor the elevator stops and someone in jogging gear gets in with their dog. Sandra's fake breast is slipping down his dress. His eyelash is now gone - the other is holding on for dear life.

"So what is going on?"

I stomp on his toe. There's people in the elevator and I can't talk.

The door finally opens on the first floor and we make a run for it, pushing the people and their dogs aside. We ran until we couldn't run anymore.

Out of breath I say "we've slept with each other a few times on the down low. One morning I had a copy of his key made while he was passed out. So whenever I see on Facebook that he and his wife are leaving town, I let myself in and throw a party."

"Bitch, I would've killed you if this is how I looked in my mugshot."

My Throat
Portland, OR – Fall 2014

I woke up on the floor of my apartment, surrounded by cigarette butts, dirty dishes, and fruit flies. Scattered around were pairs of underwear. I was unsure of which were dirty and which were clean. I'd been unable to fold clothes again. My depression had been bad for a few weeks this time. I'd started throwing dishes away. I couldn't bring myself to wash them. This morning I woke up unable to swallow. My throat was swollen. It felt like someone had lit it on fire.

Not again.

As a kid I would get strep throat constantly. My mom would always ask my doctor to remove my tonsils, to which he would say "we don't really do that anymore." I had a period in my teens where I didn't get it a lot, but as an adult it started again. I was getting strep 3-4 times a year.

My current doctor wanted me to get my tonsils out but as an adult it can be much worse, so I feared the pain. I also didn't want to quit smoking and knew the pain would be too bad to do it. I'd been keeping a log of my mental health and my bouts of depression always get worse around the time of a strep infection.

My psychiatrist had once mentioned PANDAS - neurological disorders surrounding strep infections, typically in children. I had tried to remember if my bouts of strep influenced my mental health as a child, but I couldn't remember. She didn't bring it up again.

It was the weekend and my doctor's office was closed, so I needed to go to urgent care for antibiotics. Getting to a doctor's office when depressed is like trying to run a marathon with broken legs. It's impossible. There was no way I could walk or take the bus. I'd have to borrow some money to take a cab.

* * *

I sat in the generic doctor's office. Another of hundreds just like it that I'd been in over the past few years. I was sick of going. I was sick of my blood pressure being taken. I was sick of giving blood and taking medication. My impatience came out in anger at the unsuspecting doctor. "I have strep. Just give me a prescription for clarithromycin or doxycycline."

"I don't usually prescribe either of those for strep."

"Well cephalexin and clindamycin don't do the trick anymore. I get strep multiple times a year."

"Well the strep test came back negative. I'm gonna send a culture into the lab though. I do want to start you on antibiotics anyways, there's quite a bit of pus."

"Yeah the test always comes back negative at first with me. Can we do clarithromycin?"

"I suppose you know your body better than I do. Why that antibiotic though?"

"It always seems to work faster and just makes me feel better overall."

* * *

I was researching clarithromycin and strep infections that evening and came across something called Kleine-Levin Syndrome. It was periods of psychiatric manifestations as a result of exposure to certain diseases. There were a few studies linking it to strep but nothing definitive. I gave up, took my antibiotics and some Klonopin and went to bed.

* * *

My bacterial culture came back. It tested positive for Strep Group C. Most people with infections get Strep Group A. I was told a small number of people have severe acute pharyngitis as a result of Strep Group C. The doctor wanted me to see my primary care doctor to have my throat cultured a week after I finished the antibiotics.

* * *

The culture came back positive. I was a carrier of Strep Group C. Could this have caused all of my problems? Was this why I was losing my mind? I had come prepared to my doctor's appointment. At some point in treatment, all crazy people think they are doctors. I was no exception. I'd spent months memorizing the Merck Manuel and every textbook I could get my hands on. I might as well be a doctor. I told my doctor I needed a combination of rifampin and vancomycin.

I was told no.

"I'm not leaving here without prescriptions for both."

Aside from being doctors, crazy people are persistent. Those who know us will eventually get exhausted and will stop telling us no.

I left the doctor's office with prescriptions for both antibiotics.

* * *

My cultures afterward came back negative. I never got a strep infection again. I got brownie points from my doctor. I even wrote a case study about it. The pink cloud was treacherous. My throat wasn't sore but I still couldn't get dressed. I couldn't wash dishes. I couldn't eat for days, followed by days where I would eat too much. I was still crazy. Why did I have to lose my sanity while others kept theirs? Why couldn't I hang on? Why did that cloud still follow me around?

Shopping
Los Angeles – Summer 2008

"Okay so you remember the plan?"
"Yeah I got it."

I gave him $50. I was gonna meet him an hour later down the road and give him the other $50.

"Okay. Do it in exactly fifteen minutes. Don't get distracted."

We parted ways. He walked to the other entrance of the store. My buddy and I went in the entrance in front of us. He turned left once we went inside, and I turned right.

I pretended to be taking my time, browsing the wallets, scarves, and belts. I was looking for the highest price tags and keeping note of where each item was. I made a mental checklist. It was easier for me, being in the men's section I'm sure. My buddy was in the women's section and was probably getting asked more questions than I was. He was probably telling them he was looking for a gift for his girlfriend or mom.

I began to collect a few items. Not too many. I didn't want an employee to ask me if they could put anything at the counter for me. I grabbed a leather jacket and stood in front of the mirror, trying it on.

I could hear him.

The homeless man had stuck to the plan. I could see the chaos in the reflection of the mirror. He was knocking racks over and falling into things.

I began to grab more things as the employees were distracted. They had all run away from their sections to watch the show unfold.

The homeless man grabbed a pile of clothes off the rack and tried to walk out the door with them - triggering the alarm.

I could hear a woman yell "sir you need to stop" and another yell "call the cops."

I made my way towards the entrance I'd come in at. I walked casually. Even after the alarm went off. I kept my pace, not looking back.

I'd gotten away with at least $4000 in gear.

My buddy ended up getting about double what I did, but it was my first time and women's clothes were more expensive.

We kept our word and met up with the homeless man an hour later and gave him his other $50.

We had a friend who could take the sensors off the clothes without damaging them. We still would need to pay him and then move the items.

Online Shopping
Portland, OR – Spring 2015

I'd spent months trying to figure out the dark web. No matter how many tutorials I read and watched, I couldn't understand it. All of the dealers were going to jail, as they do. It was also cheaper to buy online. I didn't have to worry about getting jumped, sitting in parking lots for hours, or sharing with the douchebag I'd just waited hours in a parking lot for.

One website had a form I could fill out. The company was based out of South Africa - or so it said. After filling out the form, they would let me know if my membership was approved or not. After submitting the form, I fell into a state of anxiety. All of the thoughts that should have come to me before filling out the form hit my brain faster than dopamine after taking a crack hit.

What if it's a setup?
What if the police show up at my house?
Or the FBI?
What if they show up to one of my classes?
What if I'm expelled?
What if I go to jail?
What if my identity is stolen?

Rational thoughts never enter the mind of the irrational until it's too late. I took a Valium and went to bed.

To my surprise, I woke up to an email from a customer service agent. Apparently this was the Comcast of drug dealing. Actually no, Comcast takes longer than a night to respond.

I was shocked at how professional "nurse baby" (the username) was. They approved my membership and I was granted access to their store.

I logged on and was floored. It was Amazon for pills. Purple pills, pink ones, white ones, tinctures, benzos, uppers, barbiturates, good ol' fashioned diet pills like ephedrine. Everything was there.

It didn't take long to decide. I would do a trial buy first. So I made the modest purchase of two hundred 2mg Xanax and one hundred 30mg Serax.

After entering my credit card details, the rational thoughts invaded my irrational mind again.

Why would I use a credit card?
Why didn't I get a visa gift card?
Would my bank trace the purchase?
Would the post office confiscate my package?
Would drug dogs show up at my mailroom?

* * *

Two weeks later I was checking the mail on the way out and I'd received a package in a nondescript brown envelope. The pills weren't concealed - just wrapped in bubble wrap. They were in their manufacturer packaging.

I popped 4mg of Xanax, and walked out the door with the envelope in my hand. I couldn't believe it actually worked. As I walked to Powell's Books, I was already back on their website, browsing the catalogue, trying to decide what I would order next. I stopped at the market and grabbed an energy drink before popping another 4mg of Xanax.

By the time I made it to Powell's, I was completely loaded. I browsed the small press section, and grabbed something with a plain cover - it matched my mood. I went to purchase the book. I set my things on the counter silently and stared at the cashier.

"Find everything alright?" She smiled.

I ignored the question and handed her my book and credit card.

She looked at me with suspicion before accepting the items I'd tried to hand her. I wondered if she could see my eyes through my sunglasses.

She rang me up and told me to have a good day.

I was silent but accepted my book and card back from her before I left.

It wasn't until I got home that I'd realized I'd left hundreds of pills on the counter at the bookstore in envelopes.

By the time I had enough money to order from the website again, it had been shut down.

The Toast
Minneapolis, MN – August 2015

We were waiting for the bus in the snow. She was smoking a cigarette.

"Smoking kills." I said.

"Fuck off." She didn't even look at me.

For three months we continued to stand near each other at the bus stop and not talk. She was a senior, I was a sophomore. We were neighbors. Her heavy eyeshadow made her look like a raccoon. Her name was Meredith.

* * *

In my apartment building we had a poolroom that was never used. I started having parties in it on the weekends. One evening we were at the pool and Meredith ran in, past the pool, into the bathroom and puked. She had taken 2cb. Her friends had trailed in behind her, and that night we all ended up hanging out by the pool. We would still stand by each other at the bus stop, but now we would say hi, and sometimes talk.

Our friendship was first based on convenience but became more than that. Ironically she would also buy me my first pack of cigarettes. I had gotten the wrong impression of her that night in the poolroom. Shortly after I met her, she grew out of using drugs for the most part – I however, was in the thick of it. She eventually became a motherly figure watching out for me. When we went to prom together that year, she scolded me for doing cocaine in the bathroom with the all-star who would go on to rob a bank. She always knew when people were bad news.

* * *

She went to college in Northern Minnesota. She cried when she said goodbye to me. I felt a level of closeness that night I'd never felt before. No friend had ever cried for me. I promised I would come and visit, and I did, a few times. She showed me how to be an adult in some ways. I learned about a proper balance between classes and going out, and remaining safe. Despite partying hard when I would go up there, there was no drugs, only alcohol, so in a way it was a break from my usual chaos. Except the one evening her roommate got so drunk and decided she'd been possessed by the devil.

We ended up locking her roommate in the dorm hallway that night. I think she was written up. This incident still seemed mundane to my usual routine down in the Twin Cities.

* * *

I went to visit her for my 18th birthday. We saw Brother Ali and Atmosphere perform that night. I ended up dancing on a side stage with her friend. We drank Captain Morgan and walked around the small, chilly Minnesota town that weekend, looking at the leaves changing colors for the Fall. I didn't feel ready to be an adult. I wasn't ready to be held accountable for my life and actions. Seeing how prepared she was made me nervous. I didn't think I could do what I saw her doing.

I visited again a few weeks later for Halloween. I wore a toga. She puked on it that night.

* * *

I was sober by the time I turned twenty-one. She had moved back to the Twin Cities. So had I, after depression and panic disorder took hold of me. One of the few times I left my house that Fall was to celebrate my twenty-first birthday with her. Coincidentally, Atmosphere and Brother Ali were doing a free concert in the cities that night. So I celebrated my two most important birthdays with her, and those same musicians. Times had changed though – in order to leave the house when I was eighteen, I took drugs to enhance my world. Now, I was taking Valium so I wouldn't be scared of it.

She told me how proud she was that I was still sober, especially now that I could now legally drink. She continued to be a support network for me. She was one of the most consistent friends I ever had. She was one who actually cared.

* * *

It was her engagement party. She didn't know I was in town and didn't know I was about to surprise her. I sat in my car chain-smoking, not wanting to do it in her backyard – she had quit years prior. I had been awake for three days. I was taking toxic amounts of Adderall. In my warped-amphetamine fueled brain, I decided it was a good idea to show up in the toga she had puked on years earlier – it had been washed but was still stained.

When I made my entrance into her backyard, she exclaimed "what are you doing here?" and wrapped her arms around me. I had a megaphone and decided to give a speech. I started it off with "The bride to be puked on this toga, that's what this stain is." I can't remember the rest of my speech, but it wasn't redeeming. All she said to me after was "why didn't you tell them how much I've grown and how I've changed?" I had embarrassed her in front of her friends, family, in-laws, and coworkers.

I got an invitation to her wedding in the mail a few months later. I can't remember if I ever RSVP'd. I didn't attend, and I never said sorry. I was too embarrassed. When I moved, I threw the puke-stained toga away, hoping the memory would go with it. It never did, and I had burned one of the last bridges standing. Nothing makes you want to jump off a bridge more than burning them.

Comfortably Numb
Portland, OR – Fall 2014

I was still sitting upright, letting the diazepam dissolve under my tongue. Pink Floyd's 'Comfortably Numb' began playing through the headphones they gave me earlier. I laid back and shut my eyes.

"Ready?" A voice said through the intercom.

"I'm ready."

The table I was laying on slowly jerked into the tube. It felt like the vibration of the table was in harmony with my racing heart. I tried to focus on the lyrics coming through my headphones. *"...There is no pain, you are receding. A distant ship, smoke on the horizon. You are only coming through in waves. Your lips move but I can't hear what you're saying..."* Pink Floyd continued to play, helping to drown out the loud humming of the machine as it conducted the MRI.

I am alone, in a dark tube, wearing a gown, listening to Pink Floyd. It's hard to believe that I'm in this situation not on LSD. Twenty feet away on the other side of a soundproof window stand a group of brilliant minds, each here for my brain. *"I cannot put my finger on it now. The child is grown. The dream is gone. I have become comfortably numb..."*

* * *

A multitude of the psychological symptoms went away upon diagnosis, showing that some were in fact manifested by anxiety. The physical ones stayed though, showing that disease did play a part in my madness. For the first time in years I could breathe. *I wasn't crazy.* I had been right the whole time. As the disease progresses, I will have a comfort that only those of us who have once gone 'insane' can have. I will have the comfort of reality. I'm not in some artificial world turning to ash. My symptoms are real. My pain is real. My reality is no longer being called fiction.

I think of what it means to be crazy, and how I had bought into this notion for so long. I think back to when I was just a kid in Los Angeles and Sophia had taken me in. Sophia was not just my exposure to mental health; she was also my exposure to the oppression within healthcare. On every street in downtown Portland are those disposed of by society – the ones deemed crazy and left to wither in the rain. It's hard for some of us to go on living, frightened that one day we could be that person sleeping on the sidewalk.

We assume that those we pass on the street, and those who are incarcerated, and the ones who are institutionalized: the people we fear, the ones we call crazy had always been that way. We assume that their present is how they have been their entire life. We blame alcohol and drugs and say things like, "they brought it on themselves," or "that's what happens when you suffer from addiction." We want it to be true, because if it is true, it could never happen to us.

So we lie to ourselves and associate crazy with images of a shirtless man singing to strangers at a bus stop. I think crazy and I think of kind and gentle Sophia leaving the world through a horrific act of violence. I think crazy, and I think of myself as a kid – happy, and healthy. No warning signs that one day my world would no longer move with the rest of the universe around the sun. Through my sickness, those that knew me had been given the reality of crazy. They watched it happen to someone so unexpectedly. Mental illness and its manifestations can begin as quietly as cancer or as profound as meningitis. Looking back, I see it, but at the time I was baffled. The start of my demise happened when I was at my best.

The truth is, the path to skid row isn't always laced in crystal meth – there is no concrete path that leads to insanity. Crazy is really just you or me and one bad day that leads to several more bad days. It's those of us who were forgotten about. Those of us who couldn't get help in time. Those of us with a disease that was misdiagnosed.

I don't have voices in my head, I don't get lost in delusions; I have an abnormal amount of CAG repeats on my fourth chromosome – in other words: a blood test said I have Huntington's Disease, and an MRI said I have a Chiari Malformation. Even with this new evidence, my doctors told me there was no reason to blame either for my symptoms, and they still believed my symptoms were the result of a mental illness.

I didn't actually need their opinion anymore – having something tangible on my medical record that could possibly be a cause for my symptoms was enough for me. It was enough to make most of my symptoms evaporate into the storm cloud hanging over my head.

Antonio Montana

Portland, OR 2003 – Minneapolis, MN 2015

The storm outside was terrible and we hadn't noticed him coming into the house. He hid in my room, soaking wet. I'm not sure how long he was in there. That night I went to go to sleep and stopped in the hallway before entering the doorway. I could see his eyes in the dark. We stood silently watching each other. I contemplated telling my mom, but I also didn't want him to leave. I wanted him to stay with me. I walked closer and he let out a meow.

I dried him off and he jumped on my lap and began purring louder than I'd ever heard a cat purr before. He was small, clearly underfed, and a little nappy. He was definitely a stray. He nuzzled his head into my stomach and I put my hands around his stomach and held him in front of my face. "What shall we call you?" I looked around the room and saw my Scarface poster. In my best Al Pacino impression, I said "I shall call you Tony."

* * *

In the summer of 2003 I lived in a car and between seedy motels on McLaughlin Blvd just outside of Portland. Tony lived in that car and in those motels with me. I turned every bathtub into a litter box for him. He never went unfed, and always slept in bed with me. One morning he escaped the motel room I was staying in. The traffic scared him and he ran off and climbed over a fence. I tried to catch him but couldn't. I stood in the cold, drizzling rain calling his name. He didn't come. My ride was leaving and the police were forcing me to leave the motel. I had to go. I'd never felt a pain like that, and had never been so consumed by anxiety.

I came back the next day. I got out of the car and before I could finish saying his name he ran up to me in a panic. He had been as frightened as I had been. I picked him up and held him tight as he continued to meow. I lost all of my possessions being homeless that Summer before 7th grade. Tony is the only thing from my boyhood that was with me when I became a teenager. He was the one thing that linked me to my old life and my innocence.

* * *

I'd had a severe case of osteomyelitis. The doctors did a biopsy of my right elbow. The pain was excruciating and I laid in bed for a week after. I had to take heavy doses of clindamycin multiple times a day for months, side effects of which kept me bedridden for longer. Tony stayed in bed with me and we listened to The Doors. I told him how much I hated Minnesota and the winter. I would take out a laser and point it at the wall for him. He'd leave my room only to go to the bathroom.

* * *

I'd started high-school, and got heavier into drugs. I'd see Tony after school and sometimes on the weekends. I often found him in my bed waiting for me while I stumbled in late at night. He became needier. We spent less time together and it was obvious he missed me. I missed him too, but that didn't keep me from going away. My family was there to keep him company.

* * *

When I got sober, Tony was the only one I showed my pain to. That dark week I spent in my room crying and craving - he never left my side. When I stopped going out so much, he was happy to have me home.

* * *

When I went away to college, Tony was my last goodbye. Every time I came home, he was the first I said hello to. I held him and kissed his head. I brought a photo of him in my suitcase. I'd Skype my mom and make her hold the cat in front of the webcam for me.

* * *

Tony got diabetes. He required one and

then two shots of insulin a day. He was constantly thirsty and needed to be put on a special diet. When I came home to visit I learned how to give him his insulin shots. I felt horrible that I couldn't afford a place while in college that accepted animals. He was best with me. He'd lost a lot of weight and his aging and health problems were obvious in his appearance.

* * *

When my depression and panic disorder got bad, I had to take a semester off of college. I had a rolling panic attack that lasted weeks – unable to sleep without Valium – I lay awake most nights. A cat's laryngeal muscles can twitch at a rate of 25 to 150 vibrations per second. When they inhale and exhale during this phenomenon, the vocal cords separate and a purring sound is produced. I'd lay awake with feelings of a stroke, petting Tony, pretending I could count how many vibrations per second his muscles were moving. I only left bed to give him his insulin shot, clean his litter box, and feed him. He only left my side to use the bathroom.

* * *

I finished college and all I had was some useless degree and an addiction to Adderall. I moved back home that summer and was unable to stay around the house. The amphetamines made me irritable and anxious - I couldn't be around people. I had to keep going. I rarely saw Tony but instead would spend my days driving around the twin cities, chain-smoking and listening to music.

Tony got sick that Summer. He lost his appetite. We were worried his diabetes had gotten worse. Just before I took him to the vet he got better. Despite him having been sick, I still didn't come home. When I did, I shut him out of my room. I was too agitated to have him jumping on my lap and demanding attention. I felt bad, but I just couldn't. I was spinning out of control and couldn't handle being touched. After a few weeks, he got sick again. My family took him to the vet without me. They'd been trying to call me all day, but I couldn't bring myself to answer the phone.

A pack of cigarettes and two Adderall later I was able to answer my phone. Tony had stomach cancer. He couldn't eat. He had to be put down. They gave me the address of the veterinarian's office so I could go and say goodbye. It hadn't actually hit me that he was dying. It didn't hit me on the drive there. It didn't hit me in the parking lot. It didn't hit me in the waiting room. When they took me back to his room, that's when it hit me. He let out a small meow that sounded like a yelp. He couldn't walk without falling over. The vet left us alone. I picked him up and I cried. I cried harder than I've ever cried.

"I'm so sorry." I sobbed and nuzzled my face into him as stray hairs from him stuck to my tears. I felt a rock forming in my throat.

"You're my best friend and I wasn't there for you. I'll never forgive myself." I couldn't breathe and I couldn't let him go. I sat in a chair holding him tight, crying uncontrollably until he began to push himself away from me, placing his paw on my chest and pushing his body away. He was in pain. He was ready to go – I wasn't ready to say goodbye, but we never are. I opened the door and tried to choke back my tears. I called to the vet "he's ready."

* * *

Addiction took a lot from me, but it never took a friendship away that I couldn't maybe one day repair. For twelve years he'd been there for me, and when he needed me most, I wasn't there for him. I'd turned my back on the one thing I loved more than anything else in this world. I finally lost something I couldn't recover: you can't turn back time and change how you spend it.

Bridge City
Portland, OR – November 2015

The Hawthorne Bridge spans 1,382 feet, resting across six piers. Roughly 30,000 people cross the bridge daily. The bridge is the oldest vertical lift bridge still in operation in the United States; it was built in 1910. It was the perfect bridge to jump from.

I watched a documentary once that interviewed people who survived jumping off the Golden Gate Bridge. The Golden Gate is much higher than the Hawthorne Bridge and the water below it colder and more treacherous. If people could survive the Golden Gate, I worried that I would survive the Hawthorne.

I walked to what I thought was the exact middle of the bridge, but I couldn't be sure. I stood in the cool Winter air debating what the exact center point actually was. I walked ten feet in one direction, and then twenty feet back in the other direction. I thought about the Vista Bridge - the main bridge people generally jumped from in Portland. The city had put a fence between the walkway and railing to prevent jumpers though. Besides, that bridge was above concrete and the thought of splattering freaked me out. Also, I didn't want to cause anyone to get in a car accident. *I can't figure out where the damn center is* I thought. Frustrated, I decided to go to the next bridge.

The Morrison Bridge is not as

aesthetically pleasing as the Hawthorne Bridge. It's really just a big chunk of concrete with some typical lights and a heavy traffic flow, but the view of the city from it is great. It goes directly into downtown Portland.

I stood there in what I was sure was the middle part of the bridge, and pulled myself off the ground with my hands on the railing. I let my feet sway for a minute before lowering myself back on the walkway.

I thought about that line in Titanic where Kate Winslet wants to jump off the boat and Leo stops her by telling her about how the cold water would feel. I can't remember what he compared it to: Thousands of knives, needles, or bits of glass or something. The point being that the pain would be horrific. *Could I handle the pain?* Who was I kidding... this was the Willamette River. I don't think the water goes below forty or fifty.

"You're being a chicken-shit." I told myself.

I stood for what must have been an hour, smoking cigarettes and staring at the city lights reflected on the river. *Would anyone even know I jumped?* There was no foot traffic on the Morrison Bridge that night. I wondered how long my body would float down the river before being discovered. I wondered how long it would take people to realize I was gone. I lived alone and frequently would disappear for a week or two at a time.

If a tree falls in a forest and no one is around to hear it, does it make a sound? If a boy jumps into a river and no one knows it, did he ever even exist?

I decided to move onto the Burnside Bridge. I didn't want my jump to hurt anyone else but I also didn't want my body to decay in a river and float downstream before someone found it.

The Burnside Bridge is probably one of Portland's most famous bridges. I can't be sure of the statistics but I would guess it's the most crossed bridge (that's not part of a highway). It has a giant neon sign that says "Portland, Oregon." Tourists like to take pictures in front of the sign. Just down the road you can find some of Portland's biggest tourist stops: Powell's Books, Voodoo Donuts, the Shanghai Tunnels.

The bridge wasn't too busy when I got to it but it had some foot traffic. Enough for someone to see me from a distance and call the police so that my body would be found before it got gross and wrinkly. I want to be cremated but I also don't want the person doing it to think I was disgusting looking. I'd even dressed up for the occasion.

I had the normal thoughts:
Would it hurt?
What happens when you die?
Would people miss me?
How many would show up at my funeral?

I thought about the cost of me dying. I hadn't thought about it before. Funerals and cremation are expensive. Who would pay for it?

The guilt of this realization made me

debate whether I should save the money for my funeral first and then die. I was out of cigarettes. There was a convenient store at the other end of Burnside Bridge on Martin Luther King. I'd walk there to buy cigarettes and would continue my debate over life or death.

There's a part in The Bell Jar where Esther has to participate in a photo shoot and she feels if anyone takes her picture she will burst into tears and won't be able to stop crying. I felt the same way; I couldn't have anyone look at me. I stood outside of the convenient store and debated going in. I couldn't handle talking to the cashier.

When I did finally go in, I kept my head down and mumbled what I wanted. It was an older middle eastern woman - maybe a little older than my mother. Before I could pay she reached across the counter and touched my hand and said "hey are you alright?"

I looked at her for a moment. There was so much concern in her eyes. My whole body felt hot and began to shake a little. I turned and ran. I ran out of the store and across the Burnside Bridge. I was crying hysterically as I ran all the way up Burnside and down Park Avenue where I stopped to puke - a combination of the tears and panting while running had made me sick. A crowd watched and as someone went to approach me I took off running again. I ran until I was home. I collapsed on the floor. *Why did she have to notice me? Why did I have to exist? Why didn't she just let me pay and leave like everyone else?*

Therapy
Minneapolis, MN – Winter 2017

Him: You say you might have Huntington's disease. Are you considering getting tested?

Me: I've been tested. I fall into what is called a gray area. I have a number of CAG repeats that is inconclusive - I might or might not develop the disease. But the thing is, there was this study done that said people in this range can have psychiatric manifestations.

Him: Is that what your doctors believe is wrong with you?

Me: Maybe. I think they wanted to give me a label in hopes that symptoms might subside if I just had an answer for why I'm so fucked up. No one was willing to concretely say that's what's wrong with me though.

Him: Did a possible diagnosis help?

Me: I don't know that either. I know I feel better. Was it the meds? Did I just need a label for my illness? Did I just get tired of going to the doctor every week and constantly going to the hospital? Maybe.

Him: Did they diagnose you with a specific mental health condition ever?

Me: Over the years I've been diagnosed with generalized anxiety disorder, panic disorder, depression, bipolar II, cyclothymia, and depersonalization disorder.

Him: And what medications have you taken and what are you still taking?

Me: I'm taking Adderall, Klonopin, Lamictal, Wellbutrin, and Lexapro. In the past I've been on lithium, Zoloft, Valium, Xanax, Ativan, Serax, Paxil, Vyvanse, Concerta, and Ritalin and maybe others I can't remember right now.

Him: What are the meds you're on targeting?

Me: The Lexapro is for panic and obsessive thoughts, the Wellbutrin is for depression, the Lamictal is for mood swings, the Klonopin is for panic attacks, and the Adderall is for derealization.

Him: And you had said on your forms that you want to discontinue your meds? Why is that?

Me: I'm not depressed anymore, my mood feels controllable, and I haven't had a panic attack in a year.

Him: You should really do that under the guidance of a doctor.

Me: Yeah I gave my psychiatrist a taper plan, she okayed it. I'm gonna stop the Adderall first, then the Wellbutrin, then the Lamictal, then the Lexapro.

Him: What about the Klonopin?

Me: I only take that as needed. I'm not really taking it anymore.

* * *

Me: I've become obsessed with Thomas Wolfe lately.

Who: Who?

Me: He was a writer, don't confuse him with Tom Wolfe. Thomas Wolfe wrote this book,

"You Can't Go Home Again." It explained my life for me. I've read it three times now.

I pull the book out of my backpack and hand it to him.

Me: The pages that are dog-eared have passages underlined that explain everything.

He opens the book to a marked passage and reads it out loud.

Him: "There came to him an image of man's whole life upon the earth. It seemed to him that all man's life was like a tiny spurt of flame that blazed out briefly in an illimitable and terrifying darkness, and that all man's grandeur, tragic dignity, his heroic glory, came from the brevity and smallness of this flame. He knew his life was little and would be extinguished, and that only darkness was immense and everlasting. And he knew that he would die with defiance on his lips, and that the shout of his denial would ring with the last pulsing of his heart into the maw of all-engulfing night."

Me: That's exactly how I feel. I'm terrified of death, but what scares me most is that my flame has started to dim but I'm still here. What does it mean if you're not technically dead but your fire is out?

Him: Your fire is still going man. You're getting your masters, you're writing every day, you're active in all of these communities.

Me: But it's not what I want to be doing... I'm just dormant right now, waiting for my life to start again. Drugs and mental illness stopped me, and now I'm scared to get started again. Here, read this passage.

I grab the book and find a page I drew an entire box around, and hand it back to him.

Him: "He had learned some of the things that every man must find out for himself, and he had found out about them as one has to find out-- through error and through trial, through fantasy and illusion, through falsehood and his own damn foolishness, through being mistaken and wrong and an idiot and egotistical and aspiring and hopeful and believing and confused. Each thing he learned was so simple and obvious, once he grasped it, that he wondered why he had not always known it. And what had he learned? A philosopher would not think it much, perhaps, and yet in a simple human way it was a good deal. Just by living, by making the thousand little daily choices that his whole complex of heredity, environment, and conscious thought, and deep emotion had driven him to make, and by taking the consequences, he had learned that he could not eat his cake and have it, too. He had learned that in spite of his strange body, so much off scale that it had often made him think himself a creature set apart, he was still the son and brother of all men living. He had learned that he could not devour the earth, that he must know and accept his limitations. He realized that much of his torment of the years past had been self-inflicted, and an inevitable part of growing up. And, most important of all for one who had taken so long to grow up, he thought he had learned not to be the slave of his emotions."

Me: I'm not doing it right anymore. There's no more trial and error for me. I've stopped taking risks. I have no more fantasy, illusion, falsehood, aspiration, foolishness, or any of that. What's a man without those things but insane and dangerously close to death? I'm not learning anything new because I'm not trying anything new. Thomas Wolfe says he learned he cannot devour the earth because he had learned his limitations. I don't know that. I don't know my limitations. For a year I've been in this routine of school, exercise, and therapy - anything to keep my mental health strong. I've never wanted to kill myself as badly as I did last week when I realized this. I have two options, I can go to the busiest overpass in the state and swan dive into the traffic. Or I can try. I can find out my limitations, and go from there - I can ignite my flame again. That's why I need to go to Cuba.

Him: Cuba? I'm not sure I'm following.

Me: I was thinking about it. It's the one place in the world I can go where I wouldn't have access to the internet or money. American cards still don't work in their ATMs, our cellphones don't work there, and I would have no way to access the internet without buying an internet card that are only good for like an hour at a time. I'd be on my own. I also can't bring any benzos with me because I can't bring controlled substances. I would have to do it all on my own, with no safety net. I know that probably sounds crazy, but I think I have to test my mental health and just throw myself in.

Him: That doesn't sound crazy at all man. It sounds like we need to get you to Cuba. If you're serious about doing this, let's spend the next few weeks planning it out and organizing. You can test yourself and be prepared at the same time. The first thing you need to do is take out that ridiculous to-do list, and delete it.

For years I had been keeping an ongoing to-do list on my phone of the things I felt I needed to do. It was hundreds of items long. All bullet-pointed. I never checked anything off of it but always added to it. It had been brought up in past appointments, but I had been unable to delete it. I felt it was a part of me now – an appendage, but one I didn't understand, like I had body integrity identity disorder for a part of me that didn't actually exist. It was holding me back. I would spend hours just looking at the things I had not yet done, would probably never do, and most importantly, didn't even make sense – things I'd written like "fix screen itch" that had been intended to be shorthand but I had since forgotten what it stood for. He was the only person I'd ever told about my to-do list. I took it out as he had suggested and I deleted it.

* * *

So we prepared. For two months we prepared. I practiced mantras to recite if panic and anxiety took over. I made sure I had enough money hidden in a shoe for an emergency plane ticket home if the worst happened. I practiced my Spanish, studied maps, and read up on Cuban culture and politics. I bought a plane ticket. I would be going alone to Cuba for a few weeks, and planned on hiking miles of the coast outside of Havana. I was also tapering off of Lexapro, Lamictal, and Wellbutrin with the help of my psychiatrist. If my symptoms came back, I had agreed to restart my meds

* * *

I'd gone to Cuba. Within an hour of being there I was robbed and left somewhere unknown by a cab driver. I almost walked back to the airport to get on a plane home. The boy of the family who was hosting me found me disheveled and upset on his street looking for the house. He was furious about the cab driver and told me that wasn't common in Cuba. I decided to sleep on it. The next morning, I went to breakfast at a nearby cafe and became friends with the entire staff at the restaurant. We went out that evening. They asked me what was going on in America – Donald Trump had recently moved into the White House. They told me it was the first time in history Cubans weren't trying to go to America. They told me about their government, and society. Mental illness came up, and they told me that suicide was a leading cause of death in Cuba. They have access to medical services, but there's not as much of a culture around medication as there is in America. Tropical beaches, nice weather, good people, no guns – but still, a high suicide rate. I wondered if there was anywhere people were happy, or could be happy.

I wasn't taking any meds. I strolled along the Malecon in Havana on my way home that night. I sat on the stone wall overlooking the coast. I tried to channel suicidal thoughts. I tried to want to die. I couldn't. I thought *this would be a beautiful place to do it.* But I still didn't want to do it.

The following night I went to a salsa music festival. It was me and thousands of others in a park, dancing the night away. I didn't blend in, and several women approached me and groped me. They offered me sex for money. After I'd been grabbed a number of times, I made my way to the outskirts of the crowd. I was approached by a guy who offered me a lot of cocaine for $30. I bought it from him. I was paranoid someone had seen and I would end up in Guantanamo Bay, and I fled.

When I returned to the house I was staying in, I poured the coke out on a book cover and stared at it. I left the room and went back outside and smoked a cigarette in the humid night air. Cuba at night is interesting. It's very lively. People don't stay in their homes and waste away before a television. They sit outside and talk to their neighbors, the kids play hide and seek, the neighborhoods are awake. *If I do coke, I'm just gonna sit and chain-smoke alone all night, not be able to sleep, and feel like shit in the morning. What if my depression comes back? What if I have a panic attack? What if I ruin all of my progress?*

I went back inside and flushed the coke down the toilet. I didn't do a single line.

* * *

I spent days walking along the coast and didn't stop until I came upon a ghost town. Most of the buildings were in ruins. The ones left standing hadn't been occupied in years. It felt like an allegory for my life. I spent two days on the beach in this town reading an old bible I found in one of the abandoned houses. I wouldn't be converting to Christianity anytime soon – it wasn't very relatable. I read the gospels and thought about my own "gospel" and those of the people I've met like me. What stories would we share that explained how the world really works? None of the saints I knew would ever be praised in the church, but I praised them. I was only still here because of them and their stories.

* * *

I was the only one on that beach. I didn't know how I would get back to Havana before my flight out, and I didn't care. I'd done it. I'd hiked miles in the hot sun of a country that doesn't speak English, with no phone, no credit card, and no plan. I was fine. I was better than fine. I was the best I'd ever been. I now knew my limitations, and there weren't many. I would run at life as fast as I could, so that if one day my depression and panic took over again, at least I could say I'd done the things I had wanted to do. If one day I were to put the noose around my neck again, I'd have reasons not to do it, for I had really lived.

Afterword – The Most American

We'd been there since morning, and it was now evening. The sun had set across my skin, from my wet, wrinkled, pale feet to my bronzed face. We would run naked into the ocean, dive under, come out and lay out so our skin could dry before doing it again. We'd told each other everything that day. Under the Mediterranean sunset, in his Spanish accent, he said "you're the most American American I've ever met. You might be the most American person to ever live."

Is he insulting me? I couldn't tell.

"Okay? Is that bad?"

"It's not bad but it can be dangerous. You see, your life couldn't have existed anywhere else. The cocaine, prescription drugs, therapy, parties with famous people, the porn, the moving from place to place, the struggles with housing because of mental illness and disease, writing a political book, the ruthlessness, all of those things are very American and a product of being an American. Your story would've been different in any other country."

We parted ways a little while later but I stayed on that beach and watched the moon reflect on the tide. In that reflection, his words repeated themselves, as did images from my life. For years my identity had been pierced by these labels, these words: addict, alcoholic, deviant, sick, diseased, dirty, slut, deranged... a basket-case. These things might be applicable to who I am, but they're just pieces of the whole picture. Everyone but this Spaniard had been too frightened to tell me what I actually am. Because the truth of what I am reveals unwanted truths about what they are: a piece of Americana - a broken person from a fractured country. I'm a product of America. I'm an American.

Platja de la Mar Bella, Barcelona, Spain
July 24th, 2018

Revelations

Is there a scale for sanity? Was I ever really insane? How insane had I been? For years I'd held onto the label of insanity as both a medal of freedom and a scarlet letter. Insanity granted me permission to do as I felt. If I wanted to take my shoes off and jump in puddles in the parking lot of a grocery store, I could. I wasn't scared of the world around me and I wasn't scared of others. Insanity had granted me liberation. Insanity had granted me permission to run through the rain naked. Insanity had also locked me in dark rooms for days. Insanity added weight to my body and then starved me. Insanity ruined friendships and relationships. Insanity gave me an excuse to not apologize. Insanity has a duality we don't discuss. I decided somewhere between Cuba and Spain that we all have a little insanity in us.

The people I've written about (myself included) all embraced theirs a little more than others. Or they at least let the world know they had embraced it (or had fallen victim to it). Like the id, ego, and superego, I think we can feed and nurture our sanity and insanity. It's a balancing act, but a dangerous one. I neglected my sanity for too long, and my actions fueled my insanity. I didn't notice what I had done until my derangement took over my life. Thousands of pills, hours in therapy, and time gave me back a fraction of what I'd lost. The rest might never come back. I might lose the last of what's left someday. In the Book of Revelations in the bible, John talks about the second-coming of Jesus. In a spiritual quest during a manic episode, I once went to confessional. I had a numbered list of all of the things I'd done wrong dating back to 1996. Somewhere around 2002 the priest stopped me. He invited me to talk with him in his office sometime. I accepted.

I expected this man to push religion down my throat. He didn't and was okay with me having no interest in the church or their beliefs. He did however explain the book of revelations to me. He said it was an allegory about balance. It was the great balance of good and evil. Something that had been around long before scripture. I left his office not believing that a second-coming of Christ was going to happen, but began to believe that a second-coming of myself could come. I would just need to learn to balance the good and the bad in my head. I've risen from the (should've been) dead more times than I can count. I got lucky, and I'm finally glad I did.

For now, I'll take my antidepressants, I'll work, I'll jump in puddles and not care when people start looking. I'll balance it, because I'm finally able.

Sound as ever.

Portland, OR July 2019

Also by This Author

Anomie in America

Out of the Woods: The Witch Hunt and Hillary Clinton

Made in the USA
Coppell, TX
16 November 2019